puccini

compact companions

PHILIPS *Classics*

COMPACT COMPANIONS

PUCCINI

JONATHON BROWN

SIMON & SCHUSTER

NEW YORK LONDON TORONTO SYDNEY TOKYO SINGAPORE

SIMON & SCHUSTER
ROCKEFELLER CENTER
1230 AVENUE OF THE AMERICAS
NEW YORK, NEW YORK 10020

Designed by Wherefore Art? Edited by Emma Lawson.

Printed and bound in Singapore by Imago Publishing Ltd.
10 9 8 7 6 5 4 3 2 1

Library of Congress Cataloging-in-Publication Data
Brown, Jonathon, 1955-
Puccini / Jonathon Brown.
p. cm. — (Compact companions)
Includes work list ( ), discography and bibliographical references ( ).
ISBN 0-684-81360-2
1. Puccini, Giacomo, 1858–1924. 2. Composers—Italy—Biography. I. Title. II. Series.
ML410. P89B76 1995
782. 1'092—dc20
[B]   95-3358
CIP
MN

Front cover picture reproduced by kind permission of Archiv Für Kunst und Geschichte, London

CONTENTS

Giacomo Puccini, 1858–1924 (Mansell)

The Problem with Puccini ...

What did the English twentieth-century newspaper columnist, known as Beachcomber, have in mind with his quip that 'Wagner is the Puccini of opera'? It deftly encapsulates the problem with Puccini: on the one hand, he seeks to put Wagner down, as merely popular, like Puccini, while on the other hand he salutes that universal popularity as the highest praise available.

It is not hard to encounter a snobbery that puts Puccini down mostly because of his popularity, a snobbery deaf to the profound pathos in his music because that same music is so memorable and accessible. He represents not quite the last of an era of sweepingly melodious grand opera in which, even where there is so-called 'real' life rather than a mythical plot, the lyricism transforms all before it, creating a magic that transcends 'real' life and can transform our own. Two other composers stand out by his side, of similar era and similar sweep (if there, however, the similarities end): Leos Janáček (1854–1928) and Richard Strauss (1864–1949), both of whom have become more of a speciality than the universal Puccini. Seven or eight of Janáček's nine operas continue to be performed, magnificent and quirkily innovative, powerful masterpieces that they are, but attract smaller audiences than the handful by Strauss – less than half his output – that remain in the full-house repertoire. Puccini (1858–1922) wrote twelve operas, of which, though four or five are marginal, another four or five are amongst the most popular, indeed 'indestructable' pieces of the entire repertoire.

This was an era in which the composer of operas had neither shame nor compunction about popularity. Writing for the theater meant writing for an audience. Opera houses regularly staged new work and just as regularly failed to re-stage new work that had not won the audience's heart. Nowadays, for instance, the Royal Opera House in Covent Garden, London, has scarcely staged a new work in fifteen years; the most notable exception has been *Gawain*, by Sir Harrison Birtwistle, who has said of the audience's difficulty with his music, 'I feel that it's their problem, not mine.' The simplest parallel today is with the world of 'musicals', though cultural snobbery dictates that for Puccini to look back over his shoulder to Verdi is perfectly apt, but that for Andrew Lloyd Webber to look back to Mozart is simply preposterous. Even the world of musicals, especially with today's lavish and expensive productions, has nothing like what was probably a rather cardboard-like profligacy of the heyday of the opera era: for instance at Turin in 1896, under the direction of Toscanini (1867–1957), there were eighty new operas in the season. One of the most successful was the first production of Puccini's *La Bohème*. Productions were briskly mounted, but closed just as quickly if unsuccessful. For example, Toscanini revived Donizetti's *L'Elisir d'amore* for Caruso at La Scala, Milan, in 1901, at extremely short notice, to replace scheduled performances of Mascagni's *Le Maschere*, which the public deemed a failure. (Incredible as it seems to us today, the Donizetti had not been heard there for over twenty seasons.) What's more, Puccini had to revise three of his operas as part of this process of survival, not only the first two, *Le Villi* (1884) and *Edgar* (1889, 1892), but even *Madame Butterfly* (1904).

Nor did that lively, claque-ridden and opinionated public balk from booing. This was all part of the world of opera as *spettacolo* – the correct term for an Italian audience's expectations of an evening at the theater. It was also an audience that had

*Giuseppe Verdi was, with
Richard Wagner, the giant
figure of nineteenth-century
opera; from under their
shadow Puccini and his
contemporaries had to make
their own way (Mansell)*

seen opera take on not quite so much a moral voice as a directly political one, during the years of revolution and unification in the second third of the nineteenth century; a voice less sermonizing than actually summoning people to their national identity and duty. No account of Italian opera in those years (and before) can be written without discussing the official censor, an office that simply does not figure in Puccini's story. Such a live atmosphere certainly gave the audience its passion for involvement with the proceedings on stage but it also explains, in the later, more frothy days of *relative* political calm, its taste for escape. Puccini was fascinated both by the brutality taken to symbolize 'real' life on stage, and the desire for exoticism.

With Verdi however, his most obvious predecessor – their careers overlapped; Verdi was seventy-one at the time of Puccini's first opera and died, aged eighty-seven, in 1901. Though the political heroism was expressed obliquely, by metaphor, not least to bypass the censor, it was nonetheless plain to the public. This partly accounts for our feeling that while the tone in Verdi is 'masculine', with Puccini the tone is feminine. (The arithmetic backs this up: eight of his twelve pieces have the heroine as their title, where for Verdi the figures are five out of twenty-six and for Wagner none out of fourteen; for Verdi, in fourteen cases the opera carries the hero as its title, and for Wagner six.) With Puccini, his world was more stable, centered on the lush bourgeois existence of the *belle époque*, a world of sensuality rather than duty and of bedroom drama rather than battlefields.

Alongside Puccini's career, however, another school of drama and opera came to the fore. Known as *verismo*, or realism, it sought to avoid the contrivances of myth and metaphor by a direct presentation of the harshness of ordinary real life, as opposed to the traditional *dramatis personae* of opera, such as gods, kings and

Richard Wagner set the agenda for opera to come, his innovation and imagination haunting Puccini more than any other (Mansell)

statesmen. Puccini, however, cannot simply be taken to be a *verismo* composer, not least because of his perfectly acute understanding that all that was happening there was the replacement of one set of contrivances with another. Puccini was very much his own man.

Verdi may seem to be the most evident comparison to make, in the case of Puccini, but it is as instructive to look at Wagner too. Wagner was born in the same year as Verdi (1813), but died in 1883. Puccini is a more slack composer and lacks the sheer range of power and moral piquancy and vision of Wagner, yet, for all its less intricate thematic web (both musically and philosophically), Puccini's music seeks flow and momentum, a seamlessness as the music progresses but also a clarity of lush sound learned from Wagner above all others. (That translucency eluded Richard Strauss, for instance, whose fabulously thick orchestration seldom has the guile or sprightliness of Puccini's.) Puccini sensed well the intoxication Wagner could induce, at a time at which, in Italy especially, much of the music-going public would be divided into the Verdi faction and the Wagnerites. In the last years of his life, as he worked on *Turandot*, almost his only directly moralizing and thus Wagnerian work, he could look at Wagner's last work, *Parsifal*, and exclaim: 'Enough of this music! We're mandolinists, amateurs: woe to him who gets caught by it! This tremendous music destroys one and makes one incapable of composing any more!' And he was to leave *Turandot* incomplete at his death.

In one department, however, Puccini could have learned more from Wagner, who was meticulous in the composition of his own libretti. Puccini never felt able to address this work; few composers have, yet the history of collaborations and contretemps associated with the production of his texts is one of almost invariable frustration and delay that held back the process of composition. He was very fussy, easily and minutely disappointed, yet also, in the final choice, not always accident-free in decision or selection.

Despite the time spent on them, not all of his texts are perfect, and in view of what we may have come to see as patches of sentimental padding lavishly wrapped in irresistible music, much of the effort can seem irrelevant in any case. From time to time Puccini may have been, in the back of his mind, quite happy for progress to undergo legitimate delays and pauses. He did not have a reputation for unstinting industry – during the composition of *Tosca* in 1896, the librettist Giacosa wrote to the publisher Ricordi:

> *You have fixed 6 December as the date at which 'Tosca' must be delivered complete, with a fine of fifty lire for every day of delay. I swear to you I am not wasting one hour. But permit me to add that Puccini wastes an infinite number of hours – whether in hunting or fishing, I don't know. I understand very well that a composer cannot start with his work until he has the entire libretto in his hands. But he has in his possession the entire libretto, and two acts of it are in their definitive form. {...} To be sure, if he wants the dialogue rendered definitive before he starts to compose, he has only to say so; but once the dialogue is really definitive, don't let him come afterwards and propose new alterations at every turn.*

In the event, the second act of *Tosca* took only five months to write; whether shooting or boating by day, Puccini had the habit of working by night. He told an interviewer once:

Puccini composed after dark; by day he preferred to shoot, fish or simply set off by boat or motor-car (Lebrecht)

Mozart and Schubert could compose amid the greatest tumult and hilarity, but I cannot do that. I have to be absolutely alone and undisturbed. Once the priest of the neighbouring village disturbed me after I had been working furiously on 'La Bohème' for five weeks. He broke in upon my solitude fearing for the salvation of my soul; but I assure you he will never do so again. I said to him, 'If you ever disturb me again while I am composing, I swear to you I shall desert the Catholic Church and become a Protestant.' I knew from conversations I had had from him that he fully believed that no worse calamity could befall me. Furthermore I added to that dire threat, 'There are other ways of communing with God besides attending Mass and Confession. When I am composing I feel that He is close to me and approves of what I am doing.' The fellow looked so puzzled I could hardly keep from laughing in his face. He made the sign of the cross with great vehemence, shouting, 'I am making for you the sign of the cross in order to exorcise the demon that compelled you to say that!'

It does not seem to have worked.

Son of Lucca

Giacomo Antonio Domenico Michele Secondo Maria Puccini was born on December 22, 1858, at Lucca, a town in Tuscany, twelve miles north-east of Pisa. His family was well known in the area and for five generations had provided Lucca with church musicians.

The composer's great-great-grandfather, Giacomo, born in 1712, was composer and director of music at the cathedral of San Martino, responding as expected to the need for masses and other ceremonial choral music. The archives in Lucca contain this ancestor's copious diaries. The great-great-grandfather, who died in 1781, had a son, Antonio Benedetto Maria, in 1747. This son took over his father's appointment at San Martino, after similar training to that of his father, at Bologna, then one of the finest academies in Europe and seat of the oldest university. With him, the family name achieved fame outside Italy. Antonio was eighty-five when he died, outliving his son Domenico Vincenzo (1772–1815); this son had also studied at Bologna and assisted his father in his official duties, but wrote operas – the first in the family to do so. These were mostly *opera buffa*, comic pieces largely peopled by stock characters. His son Michele, born in 1813, would be Puccini's father. His story follows the same mold – Lucca, Bologna, Naples too, and Lucca again, but he shone more as theorist than composer. One of his teachers was Donizetti (1797–1848) who, with Bellini (1801–1835) and Rossini (1792–1868), form the great triumvirate of Italian opera in the generation before Verdi. But it is with Giacomo that we arrive at the Puccini whose fame dispenses with the need for forename.

The church of San Michele, Lucca (J Brown)

Puccini broke the mold. His genius was not to thrive in the safe pattern that his ancestors had established. The dynastic hold that his family had on the musical life of Lucca, and of its cathedral in particular, was such that on the relatively early death of his father five years after Puccini's birth, a successor to the post was appointed only under a decree that Puccini must take over once he was old enough. Perhaps because of this fate hanging over him, Puccini made rather an uninspiring (and uninspired?) start to his musical training. To have destiny so clamped upon you, in the form of a lengthy municipal decree, is not likely to freshen a boy's outlook. Nor is the fact that the man nominated in that decree as the interim tenant of Puccini's almost hereditary post was his first teacher; who had a habit of kicking his pupil whenever he made a mistake. This was Fortunato Magi, who was also his uncle and had even taught the boy's father.

Puccini's mother, now widowed, took him to another teacher who was rather more successful, and sympathetic. From Carlo Angeloni (1834–1901) he received a thorough training of the sort designed, nonetheless, for the boy's supposed church career. Angeloni was, however, a composer of operas that were staged from time to time in Lucca. His pupil became an accomplished keyboard player on both the organ (for which he did not greatly care) and the piano.

Puccini's family was now not well off and in his teens Puccini worked as a pianist to make some money – in bars and, it is supposed, the local brothel. Such work, already in the melting pot of music and low-life, taught him the art of improvisation, both in its required fluency, to move from one jovial or pathetic ditty to the next, but also in its wit and thematic *jeu d'esprit*. Apparently, he had the habit of interweaving the Voluntary, improvised or mostly improvised as the congregation

*The young Queen Margherita, in
1851; it was thanks to a royal
scholarship that Puccini was able to
study in Milan (AKG)*

leaves the church, with folk-songs or even popular arias. It is all too easy to read any small trait of youth as the foreshadow of adult skills; nonetheless this aspect of what is to all intents and purposes his first progress as a composer perhaps became the germ of Puccini's skill in weaving a fabric of melody and reference all with a fetching, onward momentum. In maturity, his sense of progression is formidable, and can carry us, unquestioning, past some of the more preposterous aspects of the story. Equally deft is his use of themes or snatches of themes to point the direction of the drama, with nothing like the intricate dramatic as well as philosophical intent of Wagner's technique, but designed more to keep the listener in the palm of his hand. What is more, in view of his later wealth and the wranglings of his business ventures from time to time, it is amusing to note that a setting from these years of the Passiontide processional *Vexilla Regis prodeunt* – written in the mid- to late-1870s to a commission from the organist of nearby Bagni di Lucca – earned him his first income from composition: 10 lire and one of the local speciality cakes.

His first contact with opera was at Pisa, in 1876, when he was eighteen: Verdi's *Aida*. (We would call music as recent as that – it was five years old – 'contemporary'.) This performance made an impression that was to last throughout his life. Passion and endeavor grew and his compositions were from then on less in the manner of improvisations and organ trifles but quite extended pieces involving orchestra. Two years later he had written two movements of a Mass, given in Lucca in 1878 and expanded in the two following years to the full pattern of the Mass, also performed in Lucca. This gives the first signal of his substantial musicianship and brought him his first success. His instinctive drive towards opera – it was remarked upon in the flourishsome manner of the Mass – drove him to study at Milan, and for

The tower of the San Martino cathedral, Lucca,
where Puccini worked as organist (J Brown)

that he had to set himself up for the Conservatory's extremely high entrance standards. To break the family mold would require all his strength and every skill. And money.

Puccini's mother could not be expected to see her son through three years' schooling in the great city. She did, however, succeed in obtaining a royal scholarship from Queen Margherita (for the first year) as well as support from her uncle, Dr. Nicolao Cerù. He himself was a Lucca character, not only a doctor but also contributor of gossip and reviews to the local paper. The town purse of Lucca did not contribute to the further education of a talented prankster – for such he was, with a lively sense of mischief – whose musical calling was so disruptive to the municipality's traditional expectations. Indeed, he was snubbed, both in 1881 and 1882. Of course, after his death, the town took only a month to mark his birthplace with a fulsomely proud plaque at 30, via di Poggio.

With the albeit temporary and precarious security of the scholarship and the patronage of the doctor, Puccini set off for Milan late in 1880. Here he would have to pass an exam that Verdi had failed (though Verdi had been four years his junior) and which, even once passed, only allowed the student a year's grace before further examinations to decide whether he was to be granted full admission. His own response to his prospects after the first exam was oddly – and revealingly – cautious, especially given that though there were few places, he knew he had received top marks. Puccini was always shy and even nervous about his genius, and never forgot his failures and false steps. At any rate, admission did follow and lessons began, shortly before Christmas, with Antonio Bazzini (1818–1897) and Amilcare Ponchielli (1834–1886). This was no church training. Bazzini's music has been forgotten, even now in our archaeological age of radio and recordings, but he did write an opera, oddly enough on the same tale as Puccini took for his last work. Ponchielli, on the other hand, wrote half a dozen operas, of which *La Gioconda* (1876) has survived best, mostly spasmodically as a vehicle for particular singers. (One such was Maria Callas, who made her Italian début in the role in 1947; promoted not least through the efforts of Giovanni Zenatello, who had been the first Pinkerton in *Madame Butterfly*.) *La Gioconda* had been first heard at La Scala in Milan just four years before Puccini's arrival.

Perhaps the opposite characters of these two men did Puccini good; Bazzini was a stiff and rather formal sort of teacher, Ponchielli the more dynamic but nonetheless somewhat slack – Puccini could hand in work barely changed from one lesson to the next without being caught.

The contrast between the ages-old sameness of Lucca and the expanding opulence and stylishness of Milan must have been stark, and invigorating, if anything spiced by Puccini's extremely restricted means. For all he poured scorn on the standards of the exams ('ridiculously easy'), Milan was a major center. He later recalled also the hardships of those student days, more than the direct education they afforded:

Ponchielli and Bazzini, who taught me composition, thought I had talent, and my first work, a 'Sinfonia Capriccio', was praised in the newspaper 'Perseverenza', but I found cold comfort in that. I longed for all those things that money can buy and in which I was so utterly lacking. During those years at the conservatory, I suffered so from poverty, cold, hunger and misery that it embittered my soul and soured my nature. I attribute the morbid fascination that 'La Tosca' had for me to those days of penury. My diet was bread, beans and herrings, and I was sometimes so cold that I actually burned the manuscripts of my early attempts at composition to keep warm, just as Rodolfo does in 'La Bohème'.

Indeed, *La Bohème*, composed fifteen years after Puccini had entered the conservatory and telling of shanty student life in the similar heyday of Paris, is perhaps the composer's most frothily vivid and freshest in personal recollection – with or without a good pinch of salt. Recollection literally so: it has snatches lifted from the *Capriccio Sinfonico*, the orchestral piece submitted in 1883 as his graduation exercise – most notably the boisterous no-nonsense theme of the very opening. This was a life of dodging creditors, pawning coats, taking strolls between the cheapest of meals and devouring the relevant music at the piano.

The *Capriccio Sinfonico* was given three performances, in July 1883, by the student orchestra at the Conservatory. One of the chief critics of the day, Filippo Filippi (1830–1887), was impressed and while he understandably says Puccini's gift was specifically symphonic – and as Italian opera composers go, Puccini *is* the most symphonic – he does already notice the 'decisive and very rare musical temperament' and 'unity of style, personality and character'. Although Puccini was disdainful of this opinion, it was an influential and useful verdict to have received, coming as it did from an open-minded critic unusually percipient in the Italy of that time, in being a devotee of both Verdi and Wagner.

Puccini made no moves towards writing opera while at the Conservatory. He did try some vocal music, however, a Dramatic Recitative and Aria, *Ment all'avviso*, written on June 10 for his exam. It was submitted with an accompanying plea for mercy. In later life Puccini always felt a need for such a plea when launching a new piece, but on this occasion it was explicit and specific: he had suffered a toothache for seven hours during its composition.

The young Puccini (Lebrecht)

The First Opera

Puccini had made his mark; at least, on the musical world in Milan, but not yet in opera. He was quickly to set himself this larger task in a competition open throughout Italy for the composition of a one-act opera. This was the *Concorso Sonzogno*, so named after a wealthy character who had used his family's industrial fortune to artistic ends, owning both a theater and a newspaper in Milan. In 1882–83, this was to be the first of the competitions, which continued for twenty-two years. Within nine months this great lyrical dramatist's career was to be launched once and for all.

It was a daunting challenge, and put Puccini immediately face to face with another life-long challenge: librettists. The competition, perhaps inspired by Sonzogno's interest in writing as well as in music and theater, stipulated in particular that the libretto be good, not simply for its dramatic quality but for versification as well. Only in late July did Puccini land himself the services of a writer who, though he referred to the writing of libretti as 'a boring task' and would not consider it except for a decent fee, consented not only to supply one but to do so at a reduced fee (a third of his 'minimum within reason'). He was to be paid a further two thirds should the opera win the contest. This writer was Ferdinando Fontana, and it is Ponchielli who must be credited with the skills in applying most liberally the required flattery and exaggeration to lure and bargain from him both cooperation and enthusiasm. The libretto was completed within a month or so and Puccini returned to Lucca to start work.

Edoardo Sonzogno, caricatured as a man of letters. His competition spurred Puccini to his first efforts as an opera composer (Lebrecht)

He worked hard. The story is a madhatter's nonsense about love and witches in a sort of Nordic supernatural caper set in the Black Forest and Mainz. The title, *Le Villi*, means The Witches. After an extraordinary effort the score was ready on time, though it may have been sent off only on the closing date itself. At any rate, in the adjudication, it received no mention. It is also possible that Puccini's scrawl was indecipherable; he had not even submitted a fair copy.

This was not the end of things, though. If his slapdash handwriting had made the judges deaf to his skill – and in later years one of the winners, now forgotten, admitted that *Le Villi* was a far finer score than his own – his entertaining skills at the piano turned his fortune. Not on this occasion in bar or brothel, but in a fashionable Milan salon, Puccini was called upon to play some excerpts of his opera shortly into the new year, 1884, and these were received with such enthusiasm that money was raised to stage the piece: the first performance was scheduled for May 31 at the Teatro dal Verme in Milan. It was a huge success. Puccini sent a cable to his mother: *Clamorous success. Hopes surpassed. Eighteen calls. First finale repeated three times. Am happy. Giacomo.*

Within a week the great publishing house Ricordi had commissioned a second opera from Puccini & Fontana, to be given at La Scala. Soon, too, Puccini had worked *Le Villi* into a commercially more attractive two-act version, which had an immediate success in Turin at the end of the year, despite the librettist's qualms:

The singers are a lot of old crocks. The orchestra is weak and lifeless and even the baton of the valiant Bolzoni is powerless to infuse any spirit into it. {...} I may add that Puccini, who is really very patient with his criticisms, does not dare to make any more, because the only suggestion which he made last night was received with scant courtesy. The choruses are lamentably weak. At times they are simply not heard. {...} I say nothing of the staging. We have not yet been allowed to see the scenery! Puccini has little hope. I, on the other hand, believe in spite of everything it will be a success.

He was right. The work was taken up throughout Italy, at La Scala in 1885, at the Carlo Felice in Genoa in 1887, at the San Carlo in Naples in 1888. Abroad, Mahler, of all people, conducted it in Hamburg in 1892. (Rome ignored it till 1925.) In Naples, however, the reception was poor – it was booed – and though today the piece is a somewhat unconvincing rarity, Puccini's career was well and truly launched.

His life, too, had started a new chapter. Seven weeks after the triumph at the Teatro dal Verme in Milan, his mother died; and shortly thereafter he eloped with a friend's wife.

Le Villi

Act I

A spring day, in a small village in the Black Forest: villagers celebrate the betrothal of Anna and Roberto (soprano, tenor) but she is sad at the prospect of his setting out that evening for Mainz – though the purpose of his journey is to claim a fortune left to him by an aunt. Roberto makes an effort to reassure and cheer her, but to no avail. The villagers send Roberto on his way.

Act II

Roberto has forsaken Anna and she has by now died of a broken heart. Her soul has joined the ranks of the 'witches' (*villi*), girls who have died after their lovers have deserted them. Their revenge is to lure these unfaithful men to their deaths by a frenzy of dancing. The scene is set in the same village, at midnight, but it is now winter; the witches dance. Guglielmo, Anna's father (baritone), curses Roberto and summons her ghost to seek revenge. Roberto, driven by regret, has returned to the village to find Anna and at her door he pauses to express his love and longing. She appears and Roberto, unaware that it is her ghost, embraces her and joins in the dance; he is thus rushed to his death at her feet. The witches disappear. From a distant chorus we hear 'hosanna' (praise to God).

A draft of Gianni Schicchi. *The development of ideas and changes of thought can be clearly traced on Puccini's manuscripts, some of which are almost indecipherable (Lebrecht)*

New Life

It is not too surprising that the composer of *Tosca*, *Madame Butterfly* or *Turandot* had a complicated relationship with the woman – or women – in his life. That first opera sets a tone straight away. This prankish, mischievous, determined yet not thoroughly self-confident composer was somehow never going to achieve the unfettered sweep of the best music he gave his greatest lovers. Nor, once his increasingly stormy marriage had been established, was he a devout monogamist.

If it was at the keyboard that he had wooed those in the highest circles of Milanese fashionable intellectual and social life, it was also at the keyboard that he wooed the woman who would leave her husband for him and eventually, when the law allowed, marry the composer. (Incidentally, much later, in 1894, Puccini also managed by dint of his bar and brothel pianism to secure an introduction to the Contessa Blandine Gravina, Wagner's step-daughter, by chance on the same boat as he, by 'happening' to play chunks of Wagner's music on the ship's piano.) Narciso Gemignani had been an acquaintance of Puccini's at school but now, in 1884, had made the mistake of sending his wife Elvira to him for piano and singing lessons, in Lucca. They fell in love and raced off together to Milan.

Till now his worries had been at worst financial, but here began more intricate, interconnected difficulties, doubts and frustrations, to say nothing of scandal, that continued more or less throughout his life. His first opera, even including its expansion into two acts once it was free from the restrictions of the competition, had taken less than a year to write; his second, *Edgar*, on which he was about to start and which was to be only about half as long again as *Le Villi*, was to take four years. Of course, the scandal of his elopement brought an end to both sympathy and support, from Dr. Cerù especially; he asked for his money back. The addition of his lover and one of her two Gemignani children (a daughter, Fosca) and, in 1886, a son of his own, stretched his means desperately.

The publisher Giulio Ricordi stepped in with a stipend. Until his death in 1912, this man fulfilled the rôle of friend and patron as well as publisher; none of them easy parts to play. The company Ricordi had been founded in 1808 by Giovanni Ricordi (1785–1815), who had learned the arts of engraving music from Breitkopf & Härtel in Leipzig. Rossini was one of his early 'catches', and he was one of the first to see the genius of Verdi. Ricordi's son Tito (1811–1888) added a journal to the company's activity, the influential *Gazzetta Musicale*, and oversaw its expansion into one of the world's great music publishers, and one of the richest. This was the business that Giulio (1840–1912) took over, including in his duties editorship of the *Gazzetta*; it ceased publication when he died. Though his son Tito lived till 1933, the firm passed out of the family's hands in 1919.

Giulio Ricordi's support was crucial to Puccini. After the expenses of the next few years, during the composition of *Edgar*, Ricordi had to guarantee with his own money the sums the firm continued to pay the composer. Nor is his value merely to be reckoned in financial terms, for his intelligence both as a man of letters and as a musician (he published over 150 small pieces of his own, under the name J. Burgmein) made him perhaps the most percipient and certainly the most fluent commentator on Puccini's progress, as well as the most deftly diplomatic. And as can be imagined, in an opera world so prolific and so fickle, the power and risk in

Guilio Ricordi, a man of wit, charm, cunning and invention who was Puccini's most constant support and friend (Lebrecht)

such an occupation were formidable. No matter how percipient musically, such a man had also to be commercially astute. It was Ricordi's (controversial) innovation, for instance, with *La Bohème*, to publicize the first production with colorfully illustrated posters instead of the merely typeset cast-list still frequently in use by opera houses today.

The 1884 stipend was meant to last a year, on the face of it a reasonable duration for the composition of the second opera, but in the event it had to continue even after the completion of that piece no less than four years later. This stretched Ricordi's patience. Puccini, for his part, must have felt cornered. (He was also literally cramped for space in the small accommodation that had to contain his new family.) It was not, in this instance, the libretto that was to blame; Fontana's effort caused Puccini much less tinkering and dissatisfaction than was to become the norm. With *Edgar* it was the direct relationship between the composer and music on the page that was at the heart of the slow progress.

The manuscript pages were a tangle of alterations and insertions. Even after the first production, in the spring of 1889 at La Scala, about six or seven months after Puccini had completed the composition, work continued. The reception had been mild, neither encouraging nor enthusiastic, and a sort of summit meeting was quickly called between Fontana, Puccini and Ricordi. This was a tricky time. Fontana was quite (self-)satisfied with the perfection of the libretto. The critics had concentrated their attentions on the music and on Puccini's progress but on the lack of zest or spark in that progress. Guilio Ricordi had a delicate task, as he himself wished both for the work to be revised but also for Puccini to drop Fontana; since he was losing money.

The first version of *Edgar* was in four acts. This fact in itself marks the beginning of the trouble. True, it had been thirty years since Verdi had used only three acts (in *Un ballo in maschera*, 1857/58) as opposed to four or even five; and works such as *Mefistofele* (1868) by Boito (1842–1918) and Ponchielli's *La Gioconda* were in four acts, both works and composers known to Puccini. Still, it was a large step to take, to go from a successful first effort in one act to a full four-act drama. Indeed, the earlier Italian tradition of Rossini, Donizetti and Bellini had seldom gone to four acts, preferring two or three, as had Verdi except when he felt the urge, bluntly put, to compare himself with Shakespeare. Wagner had, in general, also kept to three, certainly in his mature works. Puccini had not yet learned the odd, Wagnerian paradox whereby expansive music best suits a somewhat compressed storyline. With the unenthusiastic reception given to *Edgar*, he began to learn this. It was also at this point that he first considered that he might use the play *Tosca* as a subject – a subject with essentially almost no storyline.

The second version of *Edgar* is in three acts, mainly at the cost of the last act but retaining the final scene, which had included an aria (Fidelia's lament) that the La Scala audience demanded be given an encore. (Incidentally, one tender lilting melody, discarded in this shortening, reappears in the third act of *Tosca* nearly ten years later.) Still more tinkerings followed. A scheduled first new performance at La Scala fell through and the revision was first heard in Ferrara only in 1892. This was

AMICHE DI BUTTERFLY

LA CUGINA

not the best fate for an opera from which so much had been expected. A magnificent cast in a production in Madrid just after the Ferrara performances (and after even more tinkering and the addition of a Prelude to evoke the awakening of spring), including, after much flattery and diplomacy by both Ricordi and the composer, the great tenor Francesco Tamagno (1850–1905) who, in 1887, had created the title-role of Verdi's *Otello*, failed to redeem the piece. There was a production in Buenos Aires in 1905, for which Puccini made still more revisions. The biographer Mosco Carner adds dryly, 'London heard the opera in an amateur production in 1967.' Puccini came to see the piece as a 'blunder'. Still, for Puccini's funeral Toscanini played the funeral music from *Edgar*.

Puccini lived, therefore, largely through the faith of Ricordi who, luckily for the composer, owned his company and could, no doubt through a certain dramatic flair of his own, guide its board to support his spending. Puccini's landlord was not so easily generous and served an eviction notice; Puccini responded by flaunting the night curfew and playing his piano by night – 'I go at it like mad!'

Edgar

The opera takes place in Flanders, early in the fourteenth century.

Act I

Daybreak. Edgar (tenor) finds himself with two passions, lust for Tigrana (mezzo-soprano) and a deep love for Fidelia (soprano). We see him first with Fidelia, tempted but scornful of Tigrana. Villagers appear, including Fidelia's brother Frank (baritone), who is rather taken with Tigrana, an interest she does not return. She mocks the villagers who demand she leave the village, but Edgar comes to her rescue, declares that he will leave the village with her, and sets fire to his house; he and Frank fight, and the latter is wounded.

Act II

On the terrace of a palace, at night, we find Edgar weary of his life of passion with Tigrana, and longing for the pure love of Fidelia. Tigrana is on the point of rekindling his ardor when soldiers are heard passing; Edgar decides to join them and finds that their captain is Frank – he has no regrets at the wounds he sustained for they saved him from Tigrana, as indeed now the campaigning saves Edgar. Tigrana pleads with him to no avail and swears vengeance against him.

Act III
Edgar has fallen in battle and we see the funeral procession; the crowd praises his deeds but a monk steps forward to denounce his life of debauchery. The crowd now curse Edgar, with the exception of Fidelia. Intending to throw the body to the ravens, they find that there is only the armor, whereupon the monk reveals himself to be Edgar – he embraces Fidelia, whereupon Tigrana stabs her and is dragged off.

La Scala, Milan, 1852, in a painting by Angelo Inganni (AKG)

Masaciuccoli and the Mississippi

If *Edgar* had all too traditional a dotty plot, in the manner of the taste for extravagant dramatic nonsense that was now under pressure from the more realist tendencies of the last quarter of the nineteenth century, Puccini had already, even before finishing it, come upon his hunch for the third opera, *Manon Lescaut*.

While less incredible, this can seem to have been a rash enough selection, given that only five years earlier, in 1884, Jules Massenet had taken Paris by storm with his version of the same novel. Massenet (1842–1912) had won the *Prix de Rome* in 1863 and in his career, apart from ballets and large choral pieces, wrote over two dozen lyrical operas – some find them too lyrical – of which the most famous now are *Manon* (1884), *Werther* (1892) and *Thaïs* (1894). Nor was the Massenet the only precedent; the book by the Abbé Prévost had been popular since its publication in 1731, and there had been several settings or pilferings, most notably by Auber (1782–1871). Yet of course Puccini's choice was also perfect for the same reasons. In retrospect – not least because it was performed just over a week before Verdi's final masterpiece, *Falstaff* – all of this gave the young composer an unrivalled opportunity for triumph and even cheek that sealed his reputation for bravado as much as genius. It was a mood of daring that Toscanini himself took up, incidentally, by giving the controversial, provocative first performances of *Manon Lescaut* in Paris itself only a year after the Italian première.

Instinct also made Puccini insist on having a hand in the libretto. By the time of publication however, the number of writers was so great (seven at least) and their

Abbé Antoine-François Prévost, novelist, writer and champion of English literature (Mansell)

Antoine François Prévost
Aumônier de S.A.S. Mgr.
le Prince de Conti

contributions so interchanged and mutually hacked, that it was decided to have no name on the title page. Surprisingly, the first collaborator was the composer Ruggiero Leoncavallo (1858–1915), not yet the composer of the opera *I Pagliacci* (1892) on which his immortality rests, nor yet even a man decided one way or the other between his talents as composer and dramatist. This was not the most sound choice of librettist for the young composer. Leoncavallo was Puccini's contemporary, earmarked as the most likely candidate in Italy for the next great operatic composer. Less surprisingly, he soon found himself out of the project.

There followed a writer and, at the writer's own request for help with versification, a poet: Marco Praga and Domenico Oliva. Their full treatment was completed in mid-1890. Everyone concerned was delighted. Puccini left Milan for the mountains in the north to work, returning to Lucca in 1891, where he stayed till the autumn. Everything looked settled but it was not to be so simple.

Puccini found he could work on passages for which he felt immediate affinity, especially – and luckily, for the sake of logical progress – the first scenes. But not others. It is clear from some of the letters that went to and fro that the parts he did not like were those where his writers had departed from his own outline instructions. A good deal of this 'collaboration', in reality a fidget of consternation, indignation and dissatisfaction, was channeled to the writers through the long-suffering Ricordi. Wisely so, for he had diplomatic as well as creative gifts. Most of his letters are decorated with phrases such as a plea to allow him to speak 'with my usual frankness' and with protestations of his devotion to and esteem of all involved. Ricordi eventually turned to Giacosa (1847–1906) who deflected the request onto Luigi Illica (1857–1919). But by mid-1891, a full year after there had already

*Puccini, Giacosa and Illica, seen here in
1905, a year before Giacosa's death
(AKG)*

existed a complete version by Praga and Oliva, both Giacosa and Illica were working together. It was this duo that would supply Puccini with the libretti for his next three pieces, which were also to turn out to be his most sustained sequence of great work: *La Bohème*, *Tosca* and *Madame Butterfly*.

Part of Illica's tribute to Giacosa, upon the latter's death, tells of these collaborations in fondly fraught reminiscence:

Those sessions of ours! Real battles in which there and then entire acts were torn to pieces, scene after scene sacrificed, ideas abjured which only a moment ago had seemed bright and beautiful; thus was destroyed in a minute the work of long and painful months. Giacosa, Puccini, Giulio Ricordi and I – we were a quartet because Giulio Ricordi, who was presumed to preside, would always leave his presidential chair and descend into our semicircle which was extremely narrow (two metres in circumference and rendered more narrow still and more close and uncomfortable by the mighty person of Giacosa), to become one of the most obstinate and most vigorous belligerents. {...} Giacosa was for us the equilibrium, in dark moments he was the sun, on stormy days the rainbow. {...} In that uproar of voices expressing different views and conceptions, Giacosa's voice was the delightful, persuasive song of the nightingale. {...} And Puccini? After each session he had to run to the manicurist to have his finger-nails attended to: he had bitten them off, down to the bone!

Despite, and because of, all this, in the autumn of 1892 Puccini completed the opera *Manon Lescaut*.

If the composition of this opera was all the more frenetic while the composer sought once and for all to establish himself in lyrical dramatic music, it also took place amidst (and was disrupted by) his settling into a new home. The mountains had been all very well but the presence of Leoncavallo at the town he stayed in, in the house opposite indeed, during the winter of 1890, must have been a mixed blessing, particularly as Leoncavallo was working on *I Pagliacci*. (Oddly it may have been Leoncavallo that had suggested the place to Puccini to begin with.) Puccini did not greatly like Milan itself, which was relatively close by, and began to long for his native Tuscany. The scandal of his elopement, however, prevented Elvira and the children from returning to Lucca itself and so, for the time being, she stayed in Florence. In September 1891 the family was finally able to settle afresh under one roof, in the town near to Lucca that has now become synonymous with the composer's mature inspiration: Torre del Lago.

This was no more than a hamlet, devoted to fishing and deserving of the description 'godforsaken'. For Puccini however, that is what he required, a place safe from scandal, society and squabbling collaborators. At first he rented part of a house, thereafter a grander villa, and eventually, in 1900, he had built for himself the villa that only the construction of a peat factory nearby drove him from three years before his death. With his increasing prosperity he also acquired over the years an estate overlooking Torre, and other houses in the country (for hunting especially), while retaining an apartment in Milan. His last three years were spent in a villa at Viareggio built on land he had bought a few years before.

The flatness of Torre would give it a beached character were it not for the surrounding hills. The lake – 'Torre del Lago' means the turret or tower by the lake, after an old construction still in those days something of a landmark but later destroyed – was more of a treacherous marsh; ideal for shooting. Puccini loved lost landscape pursuits such as stalking, shooting, boating in the lush reedy cover of the lake and also the then considerable exhilaration of open-road motoring. He came to like motor-boats as much as cars; he also enjoyed the hilarities and trivialities of time spent in cafés or bars. He always had this slight taste for avoiding his actual vocation. Despite a life spent between the opera houses and cities of the world, he never lost sight of his rural upbringing and the simple thrills and pleasures – and mischief – that that entailed.

One eye witness to Puccini's appearance at the first performance of *La Bohème* records that he was there 'with his rubicund face and the partly benevolent, partly sly expression of a peasant from Lucca'. True, he had rebelled against the family tradition of serving the parochial musical needs of his home town, but he had rebelled not towards sophistication but towards a rawness of earthly passion, bluntly presented, more at home in hunting gear than in frock-coat or ruffs. He had said, of the contrast between his *Manon Lescaut* and Massenet's *Manon*: 'Massenet feels it as a Frenchman, with the powder and the minuets; I shall feel it as an Italian, with desperate passion.'

The first production of *Manon Lescaut* was set for Turin on February 1, 1893, Milan being deemed too much of a risk; apart from anything else, Verdi's *Falstaff* was to open at La Scala just over a week later. Puccini reported on the preparations that, 'Here everybody is mad about it. Nevertheless the execution will be wretched because the voices can hardly be heard.' Yet there were over two dozen curtain calls and the piece was hailed by public and critics together. That had never happened before and was never to happen again in his lifetime. Within a year it had been

Puccini on the lake at Torre (Lebrecht)

heard as far afield as South America and Russia. He was even offered the professorship of composition at the Milan Conservatory. But with his newly established wealth his thoughts returned to Tuscany and to his home, and to the change in his fortune.

Manon Lescaut

Act I

Amiens. Manon (soprano) is to enter a convent and is pausing here on her journey with her brother Lescaut (baritone); she meets the young Des Grieux (tenor). They fall in love instantly.

Meanwhile one of her travelling companions, Geronte (bass), lustful of her, arranges with the innkeeper to abduct her, but their plan is overheard by Edmondo (tenor), who lets Des Grieux know. He in turn persuades Manon to go to Paris with him while her brother offers to help Geronte in his plan.

Act II

Paris. Manon has become Geronte's mistress but is weary of the life and she pines for those moments with Des Grieux. This time her brother fetches Des Grieux and the two launch into a ravishing love duet eventually interrupted by Geronte. Lescaut encourages the lovers to leave immediately but Manon wishes first to collect all her fabulous jewelry. Royal Guards, summoned by Geronte, burst in and arrest Manon as a thief.

Act III
Le Havre. Manon is to be deported to the United States, with eleven other girls; the crowd on the quayside watch the procession of prostitutes as they embark at dawn. Des Grieux persuades the ship's captain to allow him to accompany his beloved.

Act IV
A desert near New Orleans. Des Grieux has had to escape following a duel in which he may have killed his combatant; Manon dies of thirst, exhaustion and exposure.

Lina Cavalieri sang the rôle of Manon in the first production of the opera at the Metropolitan, New York (Lebrecht)

Life to the Full

With the success of *Manon Lescaut* Puccini had written an opera that had not failed to hold its head against the competition of Verdi's last. This was of personal importance – no talk of revisions and recasting the number of acts and so on – but it also made him nationally important: the succession of Italian opera was felt to be secure. In less than three years *Manon Lescaut* had been performed in over a dozen countries, reaching England and even America in less than half that. Puccini was a young master. He even felt confident enough to work for a while on two projects concurrently. One was a version of a short story by Giovanni Verga (1840–1922) called *La Lupa*, described by one commentator as 'a drama of lechery and crime'.

A feisty Sicilian author of dusty, hot prose, Verga was also by now a symbolic figure in Italian culture and the country's leading realist writer. His style is dry, not just because he uses Sicilian parched settings for his invariably tragic tales, but also because of the impersonal, matter-of-fact quality. Some of Verga's stories were evocatively, if not always accurately, rendered into English by D.H. Lawrence. It says much for Puccini's new circumstances that in 1894 he went so far as to visit Verga in Sicily and indeed took notes and photographs. (During an excursion from this trip he was arrested in Malta as a spy, having been caught using his camera.) Though he set some of the story to music, the project came to nothing. Its importance, though, lies in the new propensity he showed to look at such raw material, a taste he was to exercise with *Tosca*, once *La Bohème* was done. Indeed, his

Puccini in 1895, aged thirty-seven (AKG)

most telling complaint about Verga's brutal tale, *La Lupa*, was not as to the brutality but rather the lack of 'a single luminous and appealing figure'. This comment is a succinct clue as to why we sympathize with Puccini's work despite the still-lurking suspicion that he sought to shock. The more impossible the love, the greater the luminosity of the soul.

Hedging his bets (he wished to await the outcome of *La Lupa* in a version as a play, that in itself is another insight into his working method, his priorities as well as his doubts), he turned his attention to the second project: *La Bohème*. This gave him a subject familiar not only from his past but, quixotically enough, with his present. In a shed in Torre, a mock 'club' had been established. Puccini appears to have bought it after its previous owner couldn't run the place any longer and had to flee the country – not least because the less formally constituted ensemble of artistic types there seldom paid their bills. It was then renamed the Club La Bohème, and the following rules were instilled:

1. The members of the Club La Bohème, faithful interpreters of the spirit in which it was founded, pledge themselves under oath to be well and eat better.
2. Poker faces, pedants, weak stomachs, blockheads, puritans and other wretches of the species are not admitted and will be chased away.
3. The President acts as conciliator but undertakes to hinder the Treasurer in the collection of the subscription money.
4. The Treasurer is empowered to abscond with the money.
5. The lighting of the 'locale' is provided by a petrol lamp. Failing the fuel, the 'moccoli' of the members are to be used.

6. All games permitted by law are forbidden.

7. Silence is prohibited.

8. Wisdom is not permitted, except in special cases.

In rule 5, the pun is between 'moccolo' as meaning the stump of a candle, or 'blockhead'. As for rule 8, Puccini's *was* a special case, for his evenings spent here, blended with his memories of frugal days as a student, were distilled into what may still be seen as his least flawed and most immediate masterpiece, *La Bohème*. The characters seem to step from his very own life, if not his very own bar. As he later said in an interview with Arthur Abell:

> *I instructed Illica to construct the first setting in accordance with my description of that miserable room in which I lived when I was a student at the Milan Conservatory. Every time I hear 'La Bohème', I see in my mind's eye that bleak vista – those sordid chimney tops and all the squalor that was the bane of my youth.*

All that was needed now, to begin, was that libretto …

The original literary source for the opera is *Scènes de la Vie de Bohème* by Henry Mürger. Mürger was a young novelist who had lived the bohemian life in the Latin quarter of Paris; born in 1822, he died in 1861. The *Scènes* had been first published serially between 1847 and 1849 and offered a collection of fanciful as well as realistic vignettes of such dramatic potential that even by 1850 they had been adapted for the stage. They were fantastically popular. Indeed, it seems that Leoncavallo himself had already chosen the collection as the basis of an opera; he and Puccini happened to meet in a café in Milan in March 1893 and, whether by mischance or mischief, Puccini told him of his plans. Leoncavallo was enraged. He assumed that Puccini had stolen the idea from him. All the evidence points to *both* sides of the story. Given his already proven mischief or pluck, Puccini might well be expected to have raised the stakes and taken on the same subject as a living rival, even as that rival was at work on the idea. Equally well, he may have enjoyed their chance encounter as an opportunity teasingly to drop some hints. Yet Leoncavallo asserted the unlikely story that he had already allowed Puccini to read his treatment (he was acting as his own librettist, but these documents were usually closely guarded) and to this Puccini was adamant, he had not.

Storm. Leoncavallo had his publisher, the Sonzogno of the competition in which Puccini had tried *Le Villi*, announce the project in his newspaper; to which Puccini responded in another paper in a rather cool fashion, allowing each composer his opinion and allowing the public theirs. In the event, both composers wrote operas called *La Bohème*; but it is Puccini's that quickly went to the public's heart and has remained there ever since.

The success of *La Bohème* was dicey enough. The libretto was started in 1892, by Illica alone. Giacosa was rather too grand a figure and found collaboration not too much to his taste; nor did he like any success resulting from collaboration, since the credit was spread too thinly. However, Illica lacked flair and a poetic touch was required. Giacosa was, of course, happier to be needed, to be called up to save a situation; which was exactly the state of affairs, given Puccini's dissatisfaction. Then, having quite briskly transformed into verse almost all the libretto by Illica, Giacosa turned his own critical eye upon it and was displeased. An attempt to resign was

Ruggiero Leoncavallo, composer, librettist and, at various times, collaborator, friend and rival of Puccini's (Mansell)

defeated – whether or not it was genuine is hard to determine, but it was not to be the last. At any rate, two of the four acts were completed. Now it was the turn of Illica to stage a tantrum, to have his way over certain details. This happened a couple of times more – by now it was the summer of 1894! – but eventually by the autumn these three conscientious and fastidious artists were happy. However, Puccini had his own tribulations with the composition, as he reported in that same interview with Arthur Abell:

> *I toiled for three long years at 'La Bohème' and they were years of anguish, distress, agony of mind and soul, torment, torture and excruciating mental suffering. I was crucified. Don't misunderstand me, Mr. Abell. The ideas did flow in upon me with great ease, but to whip them into their proper shape – the shape that ensured success – was for me a Herculean task. The fourth act caused me most anguish – I wanted Mimi's death to tug at the heart-strings, but without too much drama in the orchestra. I toiled for days at that one scene and after much pondering, I decided that sustained chords would best prepare the audience for Rodolfo's heart-rending lament. I assure you that no spectator in the opera house is ever moved half as much as I was when I wrote the final notes of 'La Bohème'. I broke down and cried like a baby, so powerful was my grief.*

In December 1895 Puccini had finally completed the full score.

Quickly thereafter the first production was scheduled, for Turin, happy first home of *Manon Lescaut*, while already opera houses in other cities were bidding for subsequent productions. The first Manon, Cesira Ferrani (1863–1943), became the

Act III of La Bohème *(Lebrecht)*

first Mimi. (Ferrani – not, as is sometimes cited, Ferrari – made two 78rpm sides from both roles, in 1903; in voice a shade thinly stretched, but as Mimi with a freshness of rhythm and a smiling charm that escape many grander singers.) On this occasion the conductor chosen was Toscanini, not new to Puccini's work but never before entrusted with a first performance. His reputation was now growing not just with each season but with each production, and he commanded a prodigiously wide repertoire. In Turin he had also just given Wagner's *Götterdämmerung*, the fourth of the Ring cycle of operas. Alas, despite a good quantity of his Verdi, including *Traviata*, *Ballo*, *Aida*, *Falstaff* and at least four performances of the *Requiem*, little of his Puccini has come down to us on record – except a complete *Bohème*, which is a wonderfully free and lyrical rendering. At any rate, we can imagine what was at stake that night: nothing less than triumph would do. One of Toscanini's earlier biographers, Filippo Sacchi, describes the scene:

> *That performance at the Regio was a memorable one. Half of the royal family of Italy and critics from all over Italy were present. The Princess Letizia called {Puccini} to her box, and he stayed throughout the third act, thoroughly intimidated, with his hands between his knees.*

And yet … The reception was good but not overwhelmingly so, the critics in particular not at all enthusiastic (with one exception, in the *Corriere della Sera*, the paper Puccini had used to respond to Leoncavallo all those months before). Somehow or other, word got out, for within a month two dozen performances had been given there, a quite unique immediate success for a new work, let alone one doubted in the

Arturo Toscanini in the early 1900s
(Lebrecht)

press. I like to imagine that it was helped by a first night audience, warm enough on the evening but fired to sudden new enthusiasm by finding that the next day they could not stop humming or singing snatches of the piece – that simple litmus test by which this opera of all operas stands supreme. From there the opera has had an unstoppable career.

Puccini was now established. It is worth noting here a description of café life, as described after a first visit to Milan by Fred Gaisberg (1873–1951), sent by The Gramophone Company to make recordings on location across Europe, in the summer of 1899. It was, he says, a visit

rich in experiences that stamped it unforgettably in my mind. La Scala Theatre seemed to occupy the focal point socially and intellectually and exciting things could happen in this romantic town. For instance, after a particularly fine performance of 'Il Trovatore' the enthusiastic mob carried Tamagno to his hotel close by and there demonstrated until he appeared on the balcony and sang 'Di quella pira …'

I often saw the venerable Verdi, who would regularly take an afternoon drive in an open landau drawn by two horses. People would stand on the kerb and raise their hats in salute as the carriage proceeded down Via Manzoni to the park. A frail, transparent wisp of a man, but the trim of his pure white beard so corresponded with the popular picture of him that one could not fail to identify him …

One could sit at the Café Biffi in the Galleria and have pointed out to him Puccini, Leoncavallo, Mascagni, Franchetti, Giordano, Tamagno … as they sauntered through the throng of chattering citizens on their way to have their mid-day apéritif. Mid-day was the great moment, when the whole city converged on the Galleria. There were throngs of singers from many lands to make contact with impressarios ... to make up this clearing house of the opera world.

At last, Puccini could live life to the full ...

La Bohème

The opera is set in Paris around 1830.

Act I
Christmas Eve in the rooftop garret of some poor young artists, the painter Marcello (baritone), the poet Rodolfo (tenor), the bookish Colline (bass) and the musician Schaunard (baritone). The landlord Benoit (bass) enters to demand payment but after joining them in their frugal celebrations finds himself talkative; to his stories of his affairs the artists feign utter indignation and kick him out. They elect to continue the celebration in a café and set off, leaving only Rodolfo to finish off some work. He hears a knock on the door, and finds there the seamstress Mimi (soprano), slightly weak with a cough, seeking a match for her candle. He looks after her but as she leaves she drops her key and as they search for it their hands touch. Lovingly they exchange their stories and, arm in arm, drift off to join the others.

Act II
In the Café Momus. Musetta (soprano) joins the others, with her elderly flame Alcindoro (bass); she loves Marcello but they are apart after one of their quarrels. Still, by a ruse she rids herself for a while of Alcindoro, and she can embrace Marcello. By the time Alcindoro returns, all have gone and he is left to pay the bill.

Puccini's signature for La Bohème *(Lebrecht)*

Act III

It is now February; all is covered in snow at the 'Barrière d'Enfer' and it is dawn. Marcello is to paint the inn-sign here and Rodolfo has joined him after quarreling with Mimi. She appears and talks with Marcello but hides at the approach of Rodolfo; she overhears his resolve to leave her after these quarrels but is given away by her cough. While Marcello and Musetta resume their quarrelling, Rodolfo and Mimi make up, for the time being.

Act IV

Back in the attic of act one we find Marcello and Rodolfo going over the happier days with their respective girls. They are joined by Colline and Schaunard and their mood reaches high jinks just as Musetta appears to announce that Mimi is outside, ill and seemingly close to death. She is brought in and given Rodolfo's bed. The two recall their early love while the others go off to help in various ways. Rodolfo goes to the window to close off the light so that Mimi may sleep; but she has died.

...rdi's use of illustrated posters and covers was an innovative novelty (AKG)

Shock Horror

Strange as it may now seem, *La Bohème* was not at the time seen as sufficiently 'realist' to fit nicely into that category of *verismo* then the vogue. Based as it is almost all on a writer's actual experiences of Paris and written by a composer with not much less first-hand experience of a similarly threadbare life in Milan, it would seem to be as realistic as one can be while singing conversations in a theater over an orchestra. Realism, however, meant something much more akin to brutality and it is true that it did paradoxically inspire a style of acting (let alone subject matter) that was and can still be histrionic, stagey and unlifelike. Therefore, of that last moment of *La Bohème*, José Carreras has written:

> *A tenor who sobs, whimpers and cries probably impresses the majority of spectators who, in this tragic moment, have already been swayed by their feelings. But Rodolfo's histrionics aren't required by the libretto, nor did Puccini foresee any spectacular outpouring of grief. The tenor doesn't need to add any emotion, it's all in the music. If I can't express Rodolfo's pain with my voice, then, I'm obviously not a good tenor.*

And in this context, especially given that Puccini now felt that his next opera would have to engage *verismo* face to face, it is interesting to quote another performer's words, those of the conductor Antal Dorati (1906–1988). In his teens, he had worked with the baritone Matteo Battistini (1856–1928) who was then over seventy, but still singing 'a most urbane' Scarpia from *Tosca*:

Matteo Battistini, a baritone and contemporary of Puccini's, whose recordings are still valued today (Lebrecht)

He was as worldly and aristocratic as can be imagined. It was hard to believe that that Baron Scarpia really had to resort to tricks, not to speak of brutality, to obtain the favours of a beautiful woman. What a contrast when he arranged his own killing. He asked our Tosca to stab him in the neck, which she willingly did, using the customary rubber knife. He then grabbed the knife, holding it to his neck while he fell to the ground, and writhing in agony he smeared a tubeful of red make-up, which he held hidden in his hand, all over his face and chest. It was a gory spectacle the first time, ridiculous thereafter.

Battistini made only one recording of any of Scarpia's music, in 1911, in deep and true voice but from the first act, with the La Scala chorus. Of his excesses at that time one witness reports that 'compared with other Italian singers, he was extremely restrained'!

Perhaps the cheeriness of the poverty in *La Bohème* lacked the nastiness associated with *verismo*, even though Mimi's death has a specially heart-rending finality all the more mouth-drying for being set against the earlier high spirits. Whatever, Puccini was now looking for something bolder in tone. Again, he insisted on doing something new, even though the musical continuity between the operas is never lacking. Indeed, perhaps because of so consistent a 'voice', Puccini knew that it was in divergent subject matter that he would display variety and versatility. That became especially important now that he was established; the challenge was to take on the new raw realism the public loved.

Sardou's *Tosca* was the choice. Victorien Sardou (1831–1908) was now one of the most renowned French dramatists, already, in 1877, elected to the Académie

*Victorien Sardou, the noted French
dramatist, 1831–1908 (Lebrecht)*

Française but famed perhaps more for his 'stagecraft' than his profundity. Many of his works were written as vehicles for particular stage stars, especially Sarah Bernhardt (1844–1923), whose legendary Tosca Puccini had heard some years before, in Florence: 'I was tremendously impressed with her acting and with the wonderful portamento of her voice. It carried like a Stradivarius violin to the remotest corners of the theatre.' As a play, *Tosca* had had huge success, a drama both passionate and treacherous with a straightforward plot lending itself to monumental confrontations – of a sort still raw enough in the memory of a nation only a quarter of a century after its revolution. Unfortunately, another composer had acquired the rights, signed away a couple of years earlier by Ricordi, of all people. This was Alberto Franchetti (1860–1942), perhaps most remembered nowadays, if at all, as the composer of the music Caruso recorded on the very first 78rpm side he made. It was Ricordi who saved the situation, in a bold and modestly treacherous fashion: in cahoots with Illica he persuaded the fellow of the uselessness and vulgarity of the play, to such effect that he released his rights. We can imagine this almost *buffo* scene, of Illica, thirsting to set to work on it for Puccini, and Ricordi, thirsting to have Puccini's treatment on his books, plying nonsense and exaggeration upon the haplessly rich, self-satisfied composer – who gave in; with relief, even. Within hours, Ricordi had rushed to Puccini for *his* signature.

Sardou himself was still alive. Puccini, however, met him for the first time only in the spring of 1898, in Paris, and on the piano performed and improvised selections to show his progress with the score. Sardou knew what hot property he had on his hands – even Verdi had thought about it – and demanded a very large fee: he was bargained down to a percentage. He also took an interest in the shaping

Sarah Bernhardt as Tosca in Sardou's original play. Her legendary, mesmerizing stage presence has kept her name alive (Lebrecht)

of the opera and, a few years later, in the preparation of the first Paris production, was as enthusiastic as if he were the composer himself.

The usual ritual of going to and fro over the libretto was largely circumvented with *Tosca*, not only because of the quality of the play already but also because Illica had prepared a version for the other composer. Giacosa, brought in to add poetry, found none in the plot at all and offered his traditional resignation which was, with equal tradition, refused. Late in 1896 Puccini had before him all that he needed. Curiously, he did not really start work till the new year of 1898. It was not lack of enthusiasm, but rather the sensation of at last having earned some money and security. He was also supervising productions across the world of his now famous works. For instance, in 1897 he was in Manchester and London, on his first visit to Britain, to look in on *La Bohème*. (That year also saw a production in Los Angeles; which he did not attend!)

Puccini later recalled how for *Tosca* he found it difficult to work at Torre:

I felt the need of a more forbidding landscape for the cruel, pitiless Scarpia, and I chose Chiatri, a tiny hamlet high up in the mountains, not far from Torre. I knew the place as a boy, having spent many weeks there in a romantic, old ruined house, which my cousin owned. Later I bought it and renovated it. I had a piano sent up from Lucca and there in complete isolation, I worked at 'Tosca'. Elvira protested vehemently at having to live in such a godforsaken spot, but I found there the solitude I had to have. Elvira wrote to Ricordi, 'Giacomo is giving life to Tosca but in doing so, he is killing me.'

He also journeyed to Rome, to hear the bells that figure in the score. In Lucca it had

Ricordi's original cover for Tosca *(Lebrecht)*

been Ricordi who had exclaimed to the composer, as their talk was interrupted by church bells, 'Giacomo, with those church bells, you have the prelude to your *Tosca*.'

The full score was complete by the end of September 1899. He sent it to Ricordi and Ricordi was immediately dismayed by the last act and wrote to Puccini to say so. The composer was now much more his own master and fought his ground, refusing to make alterations. This too marks a new voice. Thus, the first performance was fixed, on this occasion, seeing that the opera is set in Rome, to take place in that city on January 14, 1900. The production was in the hands of Ricordi's son Tito, but an unforeseen problem emerged: it was all very well to reason that the setting of the opera made the setting of the première logical or self-evident, but, given that neither church nor military come out of the piece with great honor, it was a rash logic all the same. Add to that the north-south divide, provincial nationalities that persist today, as well as a new political restlessness in Italy at the turn of the century, with riots, suppression and even assassination attempts culminating in the dissolution of parliament six months before the première (and the murder of the king six months after), and it was a hot, nervy setting for a Tuscan to launch his new opera in the capital, Rome. Indeed, with the royalty and dignitaries expected for what was a national event, there was talk of bomb threats and the likelihood of an assassination attempt.

It is a wonder how anyone could balk at the violence of the opera – with its threats, torture and execution – amidst such everyday violence in the streets; but people did. The opera proved all too close to the bone and all too tragic to have immediate unanimous success, at any rate with the critics. Not, however, with the more worldly public whose reaction within a couple of performances was, in the words Schumann used of Chopin's genius, 'Hats-off!'

In passing, it may be worth noting my qualms about a performance of *Tosca* staged and broadcast live in 1990 from the actual locations in Rome that are specified in the opera; and at the actual times of day. As a puff for sponsors and singers, no doubt this was a picnic, but it is also a great disservice to Puccini, who understood that an immediacy of realism is *not* achieved with the real, and whose genius at evocation of place and time is as high in this score as anywhere in his work.

So much so, a new challenge was required ...

Tosca

The opera is set in Rome in 1800.

Act I
In the Church of Sant'Andrea della Valle the escaped political prisoner Angelotti (bass) finds refuge; moments later Cavaradossi (tenor) enters to resume work on his picture of Mary Magdalene, in fact modeled on a woman he does not know to be Angelotti's sister. The Sacristan (bass) is shocked at the picture, recognizing it as the woman frequently in church to pray. He goes and Angelotti sneaks in, to be recognized by Cavaradossi; he hides again as Tosca appears looking for the painter, but jealous of the woman in the painting, evidently a portrait. She goes. Angelotti reappears, and Cavaradossi helps him escape in woman's clothes. Baron Scarpia, Chief of Police (baritone) arrives in an awesome procession. He finds a fan left by Angelotti's sister, which makes him suspicious, as indeed is Tosca (who has reappeared), and, since he desires her, he flaunts the fan to make her doubt Cavaradossi. Tosca leaves, to be followed by Scarpia's agent Spoletta (tenor). To the music of the Te Deum, Scarpia kneels and conceives his plan to have Cavaradossi killed.

Hariclée Darclée created the rôle of Tosca (Private collection, Lebrecht)

Act II
In his grand room in the Palazzo Farnese, Scarpia is happy with his plan. Cavaradossi has been arrested and is brought in for questioning. Tosca has been summoned and, before she comes in, Scarpia sends Cavaradossi out to be tortured. Tosca cannot bear to hear his cries of pain and tells Scarpia the whereabouts of Angelotti. Though Cavaradossi is released, he sings joyously as the news of Napoleon's victory at Marengo is announced, and is then condemned to die. He is led away, but Tosca pleads with Scarpia to release him. She offers him her favors in exchange for the painter's life and Scarpia accepts; he insists upon a mock execution for form's sake and seems to issue that instruction, then signs a note of safe-conduct, whereupon Tosca stabs him to death.

Act III
On the platform of the Castel Sant'Angelo we hear a distant shepherd shortly before dawn. Cavaradossi is brought in for his final few minutes and he sings of Tosca; she arrives and tells him of the plan for a mock shooting. Their thoughts turn to their happy future. The execution squad arrives and the execution takes place. Tosca is impressed by Cavaradossi's acting his death but she finds that they have been tricked – he is dead – and just as Scarpia's body has been discovered, she evades capture by flinging herself to her death.

The first production of Tosca *(Private collection, Lebrecht)*

TEATRO COSTANZI

Sabato 20 Gennaio 1900, alle ore 8 1|2 pom.

(Sera 13ª d'Abbonamento)

QUARTA RAPPRESENTAZIONE

del Melodramma in 3 atti di V. Sardou, L. Illica e G. Giacosa:

TOSCA

Musica di GIACOMO PUCCINI

(Proprietà G. RICORDI e C.)

NUOVISSIMA

PERSONAGGI

Floria Tosca	**ERICLEA DARCLÉE**
Mario Cavaradossi	**EMILIO DE MARCHI**
Il Barone Scarpia, capo della Polizia	**EUGENIO GIRALDONI**
Cesare Angelotti	**Enrico Galli**
Il Sagrestano	**Ettore Borelli**
Spoletta, agente di Polizia	**Enrico Giordani**
Sciarrone, gendarme	Giuseppe Gironi
Un Carceriere	Aristide Parassani
Un Pastore	Angelo Righi

Soldati, Birri, Dame, Nobili, Borghesi, Popolo, ecc. — Roma, Giugno 1800.

Scene e costumi di ADOLFO KOHENSTEIN

Maestro Concertatore e Direttore d'Orchestra

LEOPOLDO MUGNONE

Maestro sostituto: TEOFILO DE ANGELIS — Maestro dei Cori: MARCO FOÀ

Orchestra Massima Romana — Società Corale Massima

FORNITORI: Scene, Società Scenografica del Teatro alla Scala — Vestiario, T. Chiappa — Attrezzi, E. Rancati — Parrucche, G. Gai — Calzature, F. Mortarelli — Macchinisti A. Pedroni.

PREZZI STABILI

3 Lire - INGRESSO - Lire 3

Poltrone Lire 15 — Sedie Lire 5 — Anfiteatro Lire 3
PALCHI: Ordine I L. 50 - Ordine II L. 60 - Ordine III L. 30

(tutto oltre l'ingresso)

2 Lire - GALLERIA - Lire 2

Bambini e Militari di bassa forza: Ingresso e Galleria metà prezzo.

Col biglietto di Galleria si accede al solo Lubbione con ingresso in Via Torino, 20.

Per comodo del pubblico la vendita dei biglietti, oltre al camerino del Teatro, aperto dalle 10 ant. le poi nei giorni di rappresentazione, e dalle 10 ant. alle 5 in quelli di riposo, avrà pure luogo nel nuovo Bar Vaccaria, Via Nazionale angolo Via del Corso.

Puccini's passion for motor-cars was to scar him for life – Elvira Puccini is seated, rear left (AKG)

Searching Far and Wide

Inasmuch as *Tosca* is considered his first essay in *verismo*, even though the relative realism of *La Bohème* makes it scarcely less fresh or vivid than Paris itself, Puccini had in this pair of works established his own separate identity. He took his time to choose the next subject. He was now an acknowledged master of world stature in the second month of a new century: what next? – and indeed, *where* next?

He considered texts by an extraordinary list of authors, including Hugo, Zola, Maetterlinck, D'Annunzio, Louÿs, Constant, Dostoevski, Balzac, Daudet and Rostand. (Perhaps in the shadow of Verdi, who died in January 1901, there is no trace of Shakespeare.) The range of tone was equally wide, though there was a leaning towards comedy without tragedy, as might be expected from the few options untried in his output. Some progress was made with a humorous subject from Daudet, but tribulations with Illica and Giacosa as well as the apparent unavailability of the rights, left the way open for a night at the theater in London to make a deep creative impression he could neither ignore nor resist. This was in July 1900; Puccini was in London for a first British production of *Tosca* at Covent Garden and during his stay he was taken to a new play by David Belasco, first seen in New York the same spring and derived from a largely true story by John Luther Long, first published in 1898: *Madame Butterfly*.

Here chance and instinct played their hand. Puccini's English was all but non-existent and his mind must have gazed upon the exotic Japanese setting and the pathos of the story in a sort of pure form. Europe was at the time enamored by oriental things – look at such disparate examples as the Métro grills in Paris, Debussy's music, or the influences on artists as different as van Gogh or Degas. Puccini immediately saw both what was utterly contemporary and timeless in the tale, its quite subtly different tone from what he had done, and its proven dramatic appeal with audiences. (That was always something Puccini wished to have as reassurance.) That night, with the playwright in the theater, he won enthusiastic approval that he could make an opera of the play.

It is easy to picture the zoo of languages as these enthusiastic men met in the theater, congratulated each other and settled the project. Formal agreement took longer to achieve however, and only the following year, in April 1901, could Illica & Giacosa set to work on what was perhaps the easiest of their collaborations. Puccini's first steps in the composition were not rapid, doubtless delayed a little by the 'research' he made into sounds and rhythms of Japan. This he pursued both assiduously but also with that disdain of perfect authenticity that would have been a superfluous distraction in an Italian opera. Progress also faltered because of Puccini's decision, halfway in, that he wished to divide the drama into two acts rather than three, as Giacosa and Illica had presented. This was around late 1902, early 1903. *La Bohème* had had four (of which one, the second, hardly propels the story and all of which Puccini preferred to call *quadri* rather than 'acts') and *Tosca* had had three, spare, confrontational acts. For *Butterfly* Puccini wanted something utterly without slack, terrifying and taut. He demanded it. Giacosa offered his resignation and it was refused.

There were then to appear dramatic events in real life that had a draining and harmful effect upon Puccini's moral and physical stamina. In February 1903 his new car crashed, at night, near Lucca. His wife, son and chauffeur escaped lightly but the composer himself was nearly crushed and suffocated by the vehicle. He broke his right leg which then received botched medical attention. After a spell in a wheelchair, it was over two years before he could walk again without a stick. He was, moreover, discovered to be mildly diabetic. He required nursing and a girl was employed in the household for these duties, a girl later to be at the center of the greatest scandal and upheaval of the composer's life. The web of later events that hang on the events of that misty night lies across the rest of his life. It was also at this time that his mistress required to be paid off — she had letters he could not afford to have published, the publication of which however she felt unable to afford to resist. And, given that Elvira's husband had died, Puccini had to have a clear life now that he could marry her, if not a clear conscience. After the legally required ten month period after her first husband's death, the wedding took place on January 3, 1904.

Nonetheless, he picked up strength enough to complete *Madame Butterfly* by the end of 1903 and the first performance was set for February 17, 1904, in Milan. (The correct title in Italian has the form 'Madama' but in English, especially given that the original play was in English, the Italian is rarely used. As for his next opera, also to a Belasco play, *The Girl of the Golden West*, even Puccini had the habit of calling his opera 'The Girl' rather than its official Italian title, *La Fanciulla del West*; though in English nowadays we paradoxically seem to prefer referring to it as 'Fanciulla'. It is pronounced with the 'ci' soft.) Under any name, the first performance of *Madame Butterfly* was a disaster and all subsequent performances were canceled.

Unlike the tricky start in Rome for *Tosca*, the trouble in Milan rounded on the work itself as an opera, on its division into two acts especially. The Italian patience is short, in Italian opera. The evening became a sort of bawdy farce and spectacle of the worst order, 'an orgy of madmen drunk with hate', as the composer called it, a 'lynching'. No sympathy was shown. One 'art-political' fault was that Puccini had been seen to prefer Rome to the north, for his première of the opera before; and Turin for the one before. Another fault lay with Toscanini, whose autocratic ways had made enemies in Milan and whose mistress sang the part of Butterfly – rather conspicuously carrying his child.

Puccini withdrew the work and refunded the fee, and set about revision, much of it following the doubts and suggestions made plain by his 'team' even two years earlier. In particular, the second act was split more satisfactorily into two scenes, in essence into a second and third act. It says something both of the relatively small though crucial adjustments required, and of Puccini's quick response and determination, that three months later at Brescia, there appeared a second version. Further small emendations were made (some of which of course the composer later changed back), as nearly a dozen productions cropped up over the next couple of years. Nonetheless, it was the main revision unveiled at Brescia that gave the work a triumphant launch on, yet again, an unstoppable career.

Even so, there was with *Madame Butterfly* more than ever with *La Bohème* that discrepancy between the public's taste and the critics' slight disdain. Sir Neville Cardus tells a nice story of this in his memoir of Sir Thomas Beecham (1879–1961), himself one of the greatest and most natural conductors of this score. Talking of his production in his Manchester seasons during the First World War, and of Rosina Buckman in the title role there, Cardus writes:

*By the turn of the century,
oriental art was highly
influential. It was valued for its
freshness and flowing sensuality,
uncluttered by Victorian fussiness
(Lebrecht)*

The stage set for the first production of Madame Butterfly *(Lebrecht)*

Her evocation of this part was quite marvellous, for she was an enormous woman physically. When asked by Sharpless to tell her age, her answer could easily have referred to her weight of flesh. Yet she was the only Butterfly in my experience who acted and played on the plane of the miniature according to the prompting of Puccini's music. Her tremulous, sadly hopeful tones, as in act II she made herself look pretty – or prettier – to please Pinkerton on his return, the way she said she needed a little more carmine to hide the traces of tears – her art elevated and purified Puccini's score of all sentimentality. Samuel Langford, music critic of the Manchester Guardian, *protested against Buckman's fine arts – 'If I hear and see her again in the part I'll end up liking the opera.'*

Apart from its obvious successes – Toscanini programmed *Butterfly* at the Metropolitan in New York for seven consecutive seasons before the First World War for instance – the piece also sealed Puccini's reputation in German-speaking opera houses. In an essay written in 1940, the theorist and composer Arnold Schoenberg (1874–1951) reports his findings for the Vienna of 1910:

When I was twenty-five I had heard the operas of Wagner between twenty and thirty times each. The average non-professional music lover in Germany or Austria could likewise claim such a record; he had heard 'Butterfly' twenty times, 'Tosca', 'Bohème', and 'Cavalleria' eighteen times each, 'Aida', 'Carmen', and 'Il Trovatore' fifteen times, 'Tannhäuser', 'Meistersinger', and 'The Barber of Seville' twenty times, 'Lohengrin', 'The Flying Dutchman', and 'Tales of Hoffman' nine times, 'Faust', 'Figaro', and 'Tristan' about eight times each, 'Manon' {the Massenet}, 'Fra Diavolo', 'Magic

Flute', and 'Salome' about seven times, 'The Prophet', 'Don Juan', and 'Freischütz' six times, 'Fidelio' four times, besides lesser known operas once or more.

The writer John Russell, in his memoir of the great conductor Erich Kleiber (1890–1951), tells this story of the eighteen-year-old student in Prague and of his distractions from his studies – almost a replay of Puccini's own student days: 'the great success of Puccini's new *Madame Butterfly* may have cut into their studies of Buxtehude and Schütz; for Kleiber's friend Friedrich Ullrich had lent him the piano-reduction – a costly novelty, at that time – and he was soon able to give a heart-rending account of its principal scenes. So devoted to Puccini was Kleiber that he wrote him a long letter and received in return a photograph inscribed *To my young admirer*. Those who have heard Kleiber's son Carlos conduct *Bohème* in that most extravagantly wonderful way may like to think he had that photograph with him.

It is extraordinary to find that it was also featured by the radical Kroll Opera in Berlin in 1931, a company associated with the conductor Otto Klemperer (1885–1973) who, with Alexander von Zemlinsky (1871–1942), Schoenberg's brother-in-law, conducted the work. (It was Klemperer's only ever Puccini.) In a theater so radical and controversial the choice of *Madame Butterfly* may have been to signal to the authorities a less subversive tone; yet no doubt the very poor light cast upon American morality (in a letter to Giacosa, Ricordi had called the character Pinkerton 'a mean American clyster [*sic*], a coward') enhanced its appeal to a theater condemned as Bolshevist. If this seems far-fetched, remember that in the political climate of Berlin then Klemperer was attacked in the streets by Nazis later that year; he made a chance get-away in a taxi.

Geraldine Farrar sang Butterfly in New York in 1907 at the time of Puccini's visit; she later recorded excerpts still available today (AKG)

Madame Butterfly

The opera is set in Nagasaki around 1900.

Act I
At a little house overlooking the harbor, the marriage-broker Goro (tenor) is showing Lieutenant Pinkerton of the U.S.Navy (tenor) the property before his marriage to Cio-Cio-San ('Butterfly') (soprano), when Sharpless (baritone), the American consul, appears. He warns Pinkerton, when he hears of the Lieutenant's flippant regard for the marriage. Butterfly appears, but the happiness is disturbed by her uncle the priest's curse on her for betrayal of her people. Pinkerton dismisses the company of relatives and friends, and the two settle into an impassioned nocturnal love duet.

Act II Part I
Butterfly is alone in the house. Three years after her marriage she has had Pinkerton's child but has had no word from him. Sharpless appears with a note from Pinkerton, who has now married an American woman but his reading of the letter is broken off by Goro who brings a wealthy suitor Yamadori (tenor); Butterfly is not interested and tells Sharpless that if Pinkerton never returns she would resume her old life as a geisha, or take her own life. She shows him the child. He leaves with deep foreboding. Scanning the harbor with a telescope she sees Pinkerton's ship and assumes he is here to return to her. With her nurse Suzuki (mezzo-soprano) she

Puccini at work in his study…

decks the room in flowers and changes into her wedding dress.

As night falls they wait.

Act II Part II

Dawn comes upon the same scene. Butterfly has not slept and Suzuki urges her away to rest. Pinkerton arrives with Kate (soprano), his new wife, and Sharpless, to ask Butterfly for the child. Pinkerton's emotion gets the better of him and he leaves before Butterfly comes in to find the other two. She understands their purpose and asks them to ask Pinkerton to return for the child in an hour. She prepares to kill herself. For a moment the presence of the child stops her but she is determined and with her father's sword takes her life. Pinkerton's cries of 'Butterfly!' are too late.

...with his dog ...

Interlude: Grove 1907

The entry for Puccini in the 1907 edition of *Grove's Dictionary of Music and Musicians* makes for a fascinating document at this stage in the story.

Of *Edgar* it says,

> *It is founded upon Alfred de Musset's wild melodrama 'La Loup et les Lèvres', the extravagant incidents of which were still further exaggerated by the librettist Fontana. Puccini struggled in vain with his impossible libretto. His music is always melodious and often vigorous and impressive, but the book was too much for him, and 'Edgar' was a complete failure. Rumours of a revised version have been circulated from time to time, but as yet the work remains buried in oblivion.*

In *Manon Lescaut* a marked improvement is detected: 'many of the scenes – notably that of the embarkation of the *filles de joie* at Havre [*sic*] – are designed with graphic decision and handled with real power.'

Enthusiasm for *La Bohème* rather misguides the writer's accuracy, however.

> *Puccini surpassed all his previous triumphs, and placed himself definitely at the head of the younger Italian composers. The librettists, Signori Giacosa and Illica, wisely made no attempt to construct a dramatic whole from Henri Murger's novel, but chose four scenes, each complete in itself and all admirably contrasted with another. {…} It abounds with simple and beautiful melodies, which do not merely charm by their*

... and driving his car (Lebrecht)

sensuous beauty, but compel admiration by their psychological fitness to the emotions they express. 'La Bohème', in a word, revealed Puccini as a composer of something more than mere talent, and his future became a matter of European interest.

Then, a new note.

'Tosca' can hardly be said to have enhanced Puccini's fame, yet it unquestionably revealed fresh aspects of his genius. The libretto {...} is a prolonged orgy of lust and crime, which lends itself but ill to musical illustration. {...} The passions treated in 'Tosca' are often crude and sometimes monstrous, and have little in common with the quick play of chequered feeling that characterises 'La Bohème', yet such passages as Cavaradossi's air in the first act, Tosca's air in the second and almost the whole of the last act, which rises to a wonderful height of lyric rapture, show that Puccini's power of expressing certain aspects of emotion was maturing in a very remarkable manner.

Butterfly, his most recent, was taken also to be the best work to date.

The score is more compact, more firmly knit, than that of any of his previous works, while its richness and glow of colour, its fine and distinguished melody, and the emotional force with which the pathetic and even tragic incidents of the libretto are treated, combine to place it very high among recent operas.

The events of that first fiasco night are related, with the dry observation that, 'the temper of Italian audiences is notoriously difficult to guage.'

And of the future?

Puccini is now in the happy position of a favourite with all classes of music-lovers. The admirable musicianship of his operas, his brilliant technique, and his fertile and varied orchestration enlist the sympathies of dilettanti, while his typically Italian flow of melody and his strongly developed dramatic feeling and power of emotional expression endear him to the less cultured classes. Whether we are to find in him a second Verdi rising from strength to strength, and developing his genius with advancing years, time alone can show, but the opening of his career unquestionably justifies the most sanguine hopes for his future.

With that something like the hopeful public perception of his career, no wonder then that he faltered.

The American Connection

Despite all these trappings of success, and the wealth that he had now started to earn, Puccini still approached the process of deciding on the next opera's text with caution. Now, after the two melodramas, he was again tempted to see how pure comic opera might suit him, to such an extent that he wrote in a letter that he never wanted to write grand opera again.

Other temptations persisted: travel, hunting, fishing, motoring, boating, and women. In London he started an affair with a banker's wife, Sybil Seligman, and their correspondence provides much of the information we have about the composer's life from now till his death. Luckily their affair drifted into friendship rather than rancor or even blackmail. Travel took him to Buenos Aires in 1905 and his first visit to America in early 1907 – in the former case to be present at a sort of retrospective of his work at which all the operas except *Le Villi* were given; and in the latter to catch a then pioneering tour of *Butterfly* around cities on the East Coast.

Manon Lescaut, *Bohème* and *Butterfly* were subsequently to be given at the Metropolitan in New York. Puccini could hardly resist. Evidently, with the American flavor of *Madame Butterfly* (in its way no less pervasive than the Japanese exoticism and indeed all the stronger for its heartlessness) and with Puccini's instinct for gadgets and cars and boats, not to mention guns, America must have seemed alive, attractive and altogether an adventure. Photographs of New York and Milan in the early 1900s could almost be indistinguishable, all trams, crowds and solid department stores; and, for instance, at the Met there were great singers with names like de Lucia, Scotti and Caruso. As in Buenos Aires, New York had a large Italian community, and Puccini could expect a huge welcome. He could not be expected to feel entirely at home, though; his next, 'American' opera was to have a new strand of inspiration from him in the homesick song of the first act, repeated rather closely in the second act of his last opera – Puccini was at heart most at home in the silent solitude of the Tuscan plains and marches. He decided to go for only three weeks but stayed five. During the stay he saw three more plays by Belasco. With that homesick song in *The Girl of the Golden West* he knew that he had found his next opera.

It was an extraordinary subject. The 'Wild West' was, after all, a recent phenomenon in American history – more recent then than the Second World War is to us now – and, for all its evident realism, had also started to become stylized in the short silent films of the time. This has proved to be an irony that has contributed (I believe) to the neglect of the piece. As an answer to the continuing challenges of 'realism' and a taste for the exotic, the Wild West must have seemed perfect: recent violent history set in still remote landscapes. For those who favored a different taste, it had even then an air of mythology, in those scratchy, jittery, flickering films and in the extravagant costumes – huge coats, tall hats, and guns slung on belts. The irony has been that once the technology of film advanced, both in the quality of image and in the actual presence of sound, cinema redefined for the theater- or cinema-going public the notion of 'realism', leaving *Fanciulla* less satisfactory, less

New York, seemingly indistinguishable from Milan (AKG)

believable, than Verdi's *Aida* – which is saying something. (Incidentally, early productions of both these operas involved as many live animals as the theater could afford.) By the time of *Gone With the Wind*, in 1939, not that much later, closer indeed after *Fanciulla* than *Fanciulla* was after *Aida*, cinema had achieved an immediacy of realism and panache in stylization that made it the natural home of 'operatic' treatment of the Wild West – and many other subjects. On top of that is the question of sound and language itself. Cinema quite happily stole from Puccini (and others) grand gestures of orchestral texture and motif to such an extent that even many opera-goers hear *Fanciulla* more as soundtrack music than they hear some soundtracks as derivative of Puccini. Whether Puccini's still quite poor English left Belasco's play as little more than a 'silent' theater experience, we do not know; however, certainly for an English-speaking audience, even without reminiscences of those dreadful 'singing cowboy' films, the libretto's patches of English and the characters' names even, make for moments that push it close to embarrassment.

At any rate, Mrs. Seligman paid for a translation of the Belasco and by the summer of 1907 Puccini had made up his mind. And despite those reservations – or my theories as to the reservations that have kept the score in the second division of Puccini's works – the composer used a more deftly colored palette and subtler techniques than in any other work before his last.

The pattern of work started afresh, this time with research into American western folk music, possibly as unTuscan as Japanese. A new librettist had to be found: no longer could Giacosa feign resignations or raise the game of Illica's prose, for after a short illness he had died in 1906. Illica was not the same without him. Instead, Carlo Zangarini was chosen, an English-speaking Italian with a New York

The opera house in Buenos Aires, at the time of the 1905 retrospective of Puccini's work (Lebrecht)

background. Inevitably, he too fell foul of the composer's fluctuating moods and requirements and needed an assistant to help him before he could present the composer with a text he could use, in the summer of 1908. After Puccini's death, Zangarini pretended that the composer was more the author than himself; we may wonder if such a claim would have been made either while Puccini could deny it, or of an opera that had had a less cautious or patchy reception.

However, just as a sufficiently final libretto may have been about to reach the composer, tragedy – and scandal – struck.

It is no surprise that Puccini was unfaithful to his wife. He liked his home comforts but he was in essence a free spirit, and the preoccupations of travel and work did not make him an easy husband; nor her an easy wife. Nor, perhaps, was the composer too detached from relishing the lurid fortunes of love and romance in his operas. He had good looks, a good sense of humor, fame and fortune. And he had affairs. It is almost certain that his wife expected something of this sort, especially on his travels when she was at home, but in the autumn of 1908 she began to tell people that Puccini was having an affair with Doria, the servant girl taken on at the time of the car crash five-and-a-half years earlier.

By now this girl was only just over twenty-one. Elvira, a wife whose volatile devotion was fueled as much by her husband's success as by his lapses of devotion, made life in the household impossible for the girl and, once she had been dismissed, made life in Torre equally impossible for her by unceasing gossip. Puccini's protestations may not have had much chance of being all that convincing. Elvira stopped at nothing and never let go, spreading talk and accusations. Puccini was decisive: he left town to escape what he regarded as a temporary neurotic nuisance.

On his return some three months later, not at all sure that he shouldn't leave his wife for good, the insults and accusations resumed – if indeed they had ever let up. Elvira was possessed enough by this to spy upon Puccini, dressed in his own clothes as disguise at night; and the composer was threatened by the girl's brother. Rumors started that the girl had had an abortion. The poor girl could stand no more and took three tablets of sublimate. After three days of searing pain, she died.

Elvira left for Milan while the girl was still on her deathbed. Puccini found that the wrath of the village turned upon his wife and away from himself once a *post mortem* examination had established the girl's virginity. The family decided to sue Elvira and Puccini was unable to buy them off. In the trial letters were made public that Puccini had written to Doria and to her mother, pledging the girl's innocence; also made public was the girl's suicide note, to the same effect. Public indeed: this was the kind of national newspaper sensation we are used to today. The case went against Elvira. Nonetheless, she lodged an appeal – she had been sentenced to prison – that was shaky in the extreme, but by now Doria's family had had their moral retribution and were prepared to accept money. Puccini paid nearly twenty times the original fine to have them drop charges.

In August 1909, Puccini resumed work on *Fanciulla*. From the past year he had nothing to show except the fraught and tragic remains of his family life. It is inevitable that the suicide seems to cast light on his subsequent work, though it is fanciful too, if not even a shade tasteless. The most evident parallel is the suicide of the slave-girl Liù, in his last opera, *Turandot*; but Liù kills herself to protect the man she loves whereas with Doria there is no evidence that her motive involved love at all but rather her honor and a sense of sheer exhaustion in the face of Elvira's suffocating campaign. The worst that can be said is that the episode seemed to have little effect upon the composer apart from the blackness that hung over his marriage; still, he made no effort to discourage an eventual rapprochement with Elvira – he knew that she could have been right, that he did flirt and have affairs; but not on this occasion. However, from about this time and for perhaps two years the composer did have an affair with a sister of a Hungarian friend of his; their correspondence was destroyed by Elvira, when she could find it – Puccini used either a friend's address or a box number. After her came the Baroness von Stängel, a liaison that lasted six years and that led the separated mother of two to ready herself to move to Viareggio to live with the composer. That would have been too much for Puccini.

As if to make up for the lost time, Puccini worked all the more on *Fanciulla*, despite the inevitably tricky relations with librettists. Guelfo Civinini (1873–1954), Zangarini's assistant, published the following in Italy, as part of a letter to a newspaper – to a Roman newspaper, moreover – shortly before the first night in New York:

> *The composer is welcome to add a few syllables or to loose some hemistich here and there for the sake of his rhythms. The music covers up all the cuts and the audience doesn't notice them. But there is an audience that reads, who also reads libretti – otherwise it wouldn't be necessary to print them – and when confronted with the final strophes of the 'canzone della nostalgia' each lengthened by two or three syllables despite the fact that it wasn't necessary from a musical standpoint, this audience may well suffer an attack of the hiccups and justifiably recommend that all those surplus feet should be applied, preferably in waltz rhythm, firmly to the backside of the librettist.*

From the very beginning, the stylized costume of westerns has made them the most operatic of films (BFI)

That first performance took place on December 10, 1910, at the Met, whose manager at that time was Giulio Gatti-Casazza (1868–1940), the energetic and devoted manager of La Scala at the time of the première of *Butterfly*. Toscanini conducted, Caruso, Destinn and Amato sang, and the audience demanded over fifty curtain-calls during the evening. Performances followed in Chicago, Boston and in May, in London, then Rome. The opera was an instant success, yet has endured less well. Puccini wrote home to Elvira:

After the dreaded evening I am writing to tell you everything. The performance was superb and the staging marvellous. Belasco himself took care of that. Caruso was splendid both as singer and as actor. The audience, rather reserved at first, soon got carried away and the success was great, magnificent. But for me it was sheer agony. I was alone during the whole first act which lasts one hour and five minutes, without any applause until the end. You can imagine my state of mind. There were over fifty curtain calls, followed by a reception in the foyer where I was introduced to thousands of people – all the millionaires, the Astors, the Goulds and so on – there was a very elaborate buffet but I only managed to drink some water. Later, at 2am with Toscanini, Tonio, Ricordi and others we went to eat in an Italian restaurant, where we relaxed and rested away from the hubbub. Reviews are excellent, with the exception of one or two who always go against both theatre and Italians. They call me the Belasco of opera. They all publish my ugly face. Profits from the première amounted to 112,000 lire.

Caruso's caricature of himself as Dick Johnson in La
Fanciulla del West *(Lebrecht)*

La Fanciulla del West

The opera is set in the Californian mountains during the gold rush of 1849–50

Act I
In the 'Polka' saloon miners are making merry. Rance (baritone), the sheriff, is told that Wells Fargo is looking for Ramerrez, whose gang has been threatening the neighborhood. Minnie (soprano) arrives. As she commences her Bible class, she resists Rance's attentions. A stranger appears, Dick Johnson (tenor), who recognizes Minnie as a girl he loved long ago. One of Ramerrez's men is brought in and tells the sheriff he will lead him to the bandit's hideout; they all go; but it is a ruse, for the man had recognized Johnson to be Ramerrez. Minnie and Dick talk. His love rekindled, he decides not to steal the gold in her trust; she for her part invites him to her cabin.

Act II
Minnie makes ready for her visitor, who comes. They declare their love. He hides when the sheriff and his posse appear, having followed the trail. She protests that she is alone and sends them away, but when they are gone she rounds on Johnson/Ramerrez; to which he tells her his sad story. He goes, and is immediately shot; Minnie takes him in, hides him and persuades the sheriff that he had escaped. This ruse is foiled by drops of blood from the wounded bandit hiding in the loft. Minnie makes a deal with the sheriff, gambling their lives

on a game of cards. She cheats and wins.

Act III

It is dawn in the forest. Johnson/Ramerrez, now recovered, is to be lynched by the miners. He hopes that Minnie will be spared news of his ignominious end, whereupon she comes upon the scene and pleads for his life. Jealous as he is, Rance cannot deflect her purpose and the lovers leave for a new life.

Maria Jeriza was a strong and popular – not to say controversial – interpreter of Puccini's music. Here she is seen with Hofbauer and Piccaver in a production of Fanciulla *(Lebrecht)*

Dither and Experiment

In 1911 Puccini wrote to Mrs. Seligman, 'I have a desire to laugh and to make people laugh.' No wonder, after the subjects of so many of his operas and the events of his life. The years after *Fanciulla* were restless, not just with travel but also with a particularly undecided search for the next libretto. Many blind alleys were explored, Seligman even translating a German play for him. Giuseppe Adami (1878–1946) spent a year working up a Spanish comedy but by 1913 no more of this was heard, though their friendship and collaboration lasted till the composer's death. In 1912 D'Annunzio (1863–1938) even wrote him a libretto – for the congruency of their great reputations, such a collaboration was sometimes mooted if only for its heavyweight quality, but D'Annunzio's style was already too sensual to lend itself to Puccini's already sensual music. So, there was no lack of suggestions; but nothing seemed right.

It was also the era of 'modern' music by this time, marked most of all for us by the first performance of Stravinsky's *The Rite of Spring* in 1913. Puccini, no doubt conscious of his continuing an ancient tradition of spectacle and music-drama, had no qualms about the validity of this (though it is unlikely he would have seen or would have wished to see himself as quite the last of his own tradition); but equally he was aware that he was now not the once contemporary of old Verdi's last masterpiece but also the actual contemporary of first performances of masterpieces by Debussy (1862–1918) – quite an influence in *Fanciulla* – Richard Strauss (1864–1939) and even Schoenberg. Filippo Sacchi tells this story:

To the outside world, Puccini seemed calmly assured, as in this caricature by Lindloff; but privately this was not the case (AKG)

Puccini's last years were also embittered by the negative and almost contemptuous attitude towards him of the younger generation of Italian musicians and critics. That they should think and say of him that he was just a talented melody-maker {...} without any real culture and without anything essential to say, drove him almost to desperation. {...} One evening, coming out from a performance of 'Deborah', Gaianus, who was then music critic on the 'Resto del Carlino', noticed a solitary figure at a table at one of the cafés in the Galleria. On looking more closely, he recognised Puccini. He joined him, and they sat talking until two in the morning. Puccini poured out his grievances. {...} At one point in the conversation he made the following naïve and moving statement: 'When you come to Viareggio, I will show you my scores of Debussy, Strauss, Dukas, and others. You will see how worn they are, because I have read, re-read, analysed, and made notes all over them ...' He, the composer performed more than anyone else in the world, was trying to make excuses for himself.

Indeed, Schoenberg held Puccini's talent in high regard and was complimented by his presence at a performance of his eerie and expressionist *Pierrot Lunaire*. That was a few years later, but it illustrates well Puccini's own outlook. In a book entitled *The Language of Modern Music*, Donald Mitchell puts this nicely when discussing the generally hostile reaction to Schoenberg's music:

But even if one takes a composer as remote from Schoenberg as Puccini, one still meets the understanding that matters, the feeling, as obscured as it doubtless must have been by inevitable antipathies, that this – Puccini, in 1923, heard 'Pierrot Lunaire' conducted by Schoenberg in Florence – was an essentially creative voice of unusual significance.

By the First World War, Richard Strauss had established himself as a bold and shocking innovator in opera (Mansell)

'*Who can say that Schoenberg will not be a point of departure to a goal in the distant future? But at present – unless I understand nothing – we are as far from a concrete artistic realisation of it as Mars is from Earth.*' Puccini may have been bewildered but he was not, it seems, hostile. And there were many who, with a musical equipment which could not be mentioned in the same breath as Puccini's, were prepared to say outright that the idea of Schoenberg as a '*point of departure to a goal in the distant future*' was both ludicrous and lunatic.

Puccini for his part nonetheless found *The Rite of Spring* the 'stuff of a madman' and Strauss's *Elektra* 'a horror'. Puccini wished to be an innovator, but in his own way. It is fair to say that though his musical language grew and his orchestration became ever more elusive and supple, he also recycled all sorts of effects, timbres and even melodies from one decade to the next; it was more as man of the theater that his innovations make sense – in the choice of subject especially. On this front there was certainly a great deal of dither in these years, not helped by the death of Ricordi whose schemes, service and sheer insight and shrewdness had often focused Puccini at the right moment. Tito inherited the company but not these qualities. And from these years came two flawed small-scale experiments which might stand proof enough of the necessity of grandeur, in passion and in setting, in Puccini's greatest work, were he never to have triumphed in his last work, the masterpiece, *Turandot*.

A caricature of his own head by Puccini (Lebrecht)

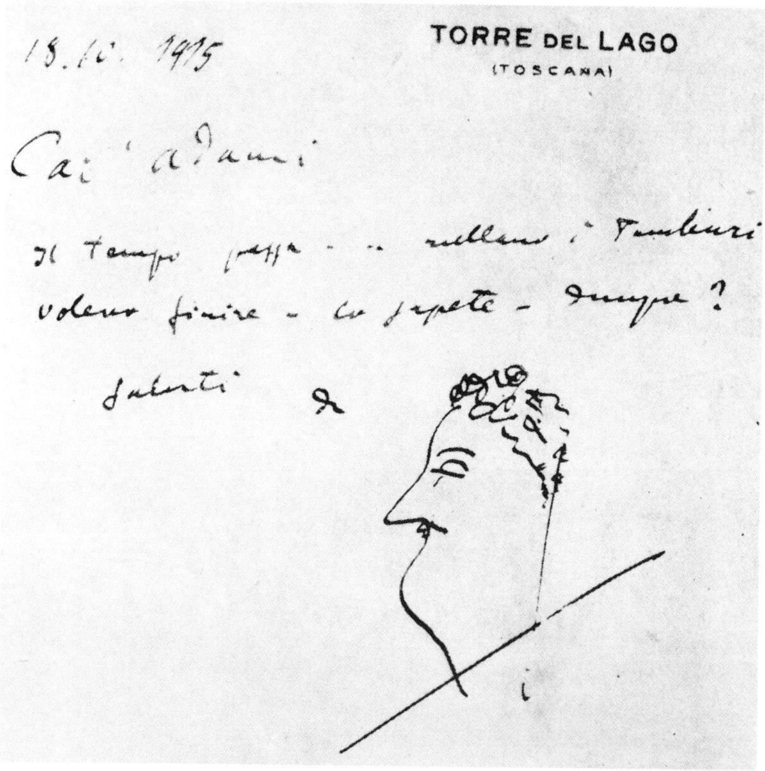

The experiments consisted first of an operetta, *La Rondine*, then a set of three one-act operas. These were composed against the backdrop of the disintegrating mood of European politics and the First World War itself. If we expect Puccini to try to shelter from the war at his desk nonetheless we find him, in 1914, concluding a (lucrative) contract for the operetta with a consortium of Viennese representing the Karl Theater – Viennese who would find themselves a year later on opposing sides of the war. Puccini, in his way, tried to unthink the war. His hedging public statements of neutrality or impartiality simply caused him almost more approbrium than if he had planted his feet firmly on either side, no matter which. He did write a piano piece and a song whose sales benefited two Italian war charities, but perhaps his most substantial effort benefited a French fund, namely the donation of a year's royalties from performances of *Tosca* in Paris. His 'Hymn to Rome', commissioned to celebrate Italian successes, earned *him* a gold watch – he considered the piece to be 'pig-swill'. His mixture of disinterest and vacillation caused friction with Toscanini, whose morality was cast in vigorous black and white and whose principles were clear and firm. Their friendship was at this time in abeyance.

By dint of meetings in Switzerland to keep the collaborations on the go (as well as his affair with the Baroness von Strängel), Puccini altered all aspects of the commission to suit himself, undeterred in his usual finickying by a Europe that was tearing itself limb from limb. It is a strange aspect of that war that so many people could imagine that it was either to be short-lived or to be fought by others. At any rate, he had possibly been tempted by the fee and royalties, truly enormous, but he had all the same accepted not to write continuous music for the text, but, as in the proper nature of the genre itself, 'numbers', interspersed in spoken dialogue. This

*Puccini by Ludwig
Nauer, 1913
(AKG)*

was clearly quite an experiment, against the grain – Puccini hardly wrote any songs, let alone anything under half an hour's continuous music – but he won his request to recast the thing as a continuous score; with Adami's help, though the contract had stipulated Austrian writers. The piece was finished a year later, in 1916, too soon for it to appear, as stipulated, for its first performance in what was still the enemy capital, Vienna.

The score languished only a year, however, for the publisher Sonzogno – himself son and heir of the publisher who had sponsored the competition all those years before – bought the rights from the Austrians and staged it, not in Italy but in Monte Carlo, in March 1917. The piece was well received; the cast included the irresistibly charming Tito Schipa. Perhaps, however, the enthusiasm has to be seen in the context of war, for since that time the piece has seldom been offered and has existed as a curiosity more than anything else.

The other 'experiment', to speak so of this patchy period of untypical works, was a set of three one-act operas called *Il trittico*, the triptych. Composition had started on one of the three in 1913 but the business of the operetta interrupted this till 1915; even then the subject matter of the other two had not been decided. Puccini expected Adami to come up with the inspiration for these but he did not and he found that two suggestions from a young writer chimed perfectly: this was Giovacchino Forzano (1884–1970). One wonders how Puccini's life might have gone if he had found rather earlier as he had at last here, a solitary writer who worked quickly and well. It may also be wondered why he seemed incapable of originating a plot himself.

Though Wagner's characters come for the most part from mythology, they serve a very clear moral function in an almost relentless succession of operas that investigate the nature of love. Wagner's genius is manifest in his decisive boldness (and eroticism) and sense of progress. Puccini had little of this and for all his efforts to do something new or novel, there is little sense of actual moral progress between the pieces. Until the last. It is an odd shyness or fear even, in a man so consummately a 'man of the theater', and is part of the make-up of a man whose theme is so often the brutally thwarted passion of love and in whose work we can sometimes glimpse something akin to the futility of love. Indeed, the 'futility of love' links more of his works than any other notion, yet this too may be part of that Puccini problem – Wagner, for instance, would have found such a notion well nigh immoral. And so it may be that underlying the Puccini problem is our instinct that no matter how well expressed or colored-in, the artist must go beyond stating such futility, to denying it. He has to take sides. This Puccini had not quite done, till his last work. I am inclined to see the unsatisfactory output of these war years, let alone in the context of Puccini's unsatisfactory personal past love-life, as a summoning for instincts and moral boldness that were only then to be triumphed in *Turandot*.

Only in the last scene of that last work does Puccini stand forward from theater into the light of belief. For now, in *Suor Angelica*, the centerpiece of *Il Trittico*, the final vision of angels and the Virgin may be said briefly not to work either as theater, morality or music. Obstinately, Puccini regarded *Suor Angelica* as the best of the three, an opinion likely to have been wishful thinking based simply on the fact it is not true – for in *Gianni Schicchi*, in presentation the third of the set, the composer at last achieved a comic masterpiece indeed, a tour-de-force whose story comes from just a couple of lines in Dante. As for *Il Tabarro*, this vignette of violence that opens the evening is an under-performed but fine piece of work, almost as if Puccini were restoring his faith in his powers of description and in his description of harsh power. (As a 'modern' touch, the score includes a motor horn.) The threesome is seldom performed as a set now. Puccini did not like the pieces to be given separately, nor did he like one to be dropped (especially as it was usually *Suor Angelica*). But it is a demanding evening, however, not only for the audience, since the pieces are between fifty minutes and an hour each, but also for the production purse. Yet as a set they can be seen as a rehearsal of three skills that were to be transformed in *Turandot*: brutality, some comedy, but also transcendence.

Not least because of the chaos in Europe, it was New York that won the première of *Il trittico* and the Met did the occasion proud, with Claudia Muzio, Giulio Crimi, Giuseppe De Luca, Geraldine Farrar and Florence Easton in the casts. Puccini was unable to attend. The reception was not enthusiastic, nor damning, though the quality of *Gianni Schicchi* was recognized. Toscanini thought the whole thing lamentable, which did not speed the old friends' reconciliation.

In all of them, one thing is missing: magic – and this had to be rectified just as Puccini's live reputation had to be rescuscitated.

La Rondine

The action is set in Paris during the Second Empire.

Act I

A party at the magnificent house of Magda de Civry (soprano) is in full swing. Prunier (tenor), a poet, laughs at the fashion for romantic love and his hostess recalls her love for a young student long ago. Ruggero (tenor) appears; he is the son of a friend of Rambaldo (Magda's lover) (baritone) and is here on his first trip to Paris. Lisette (soprano) suggests they visit the 'Chez Bullier'; this being the location of Magda's first love, she goes too.

Act II

Students are waltzing at Bullier's. Magda is dressed as a servant. To evade attention paid to her she claims to have a rendezvous and goes to Ruggero's table; he does not recognize her, but they fall in love.

Act III

They live together in happiness for a few months and we find them in their home overlooking the Mediterranean. He wishes to marry her. He has asked his mother for permission but Magda declares that her past renders her unfit and she leaves to return to Rambaldo.

Il Trittico

I: IL TABARRO

The action is set in Paris in the early 1900s, on a barge. Giorgetta (soprano) has a husband, Michele (baritone) and a lover, Luigi (tenor). Luigi is a steward on the barge and declares that he intends leaving it at Rouen. Michele, the captain, goes below, and the unhappy lovers arrange their usual rendezvous and the usual signal – the lighting of a match. He goes and Michele returns. He recalls the early days of their love and how he used to shield her with his great cloak (*tabarro*). Giorgetta goes below. Michele, alone, ponders who might be his wife's lover; he eliminates Luigi as a suspect but, lighting his pipe, inadvertantly gives Luigi Giorgetta's signal. Luigi rushes on board and Michele extracts a confession and strangles him. He hides the body under his cloak. Giorgetta appears and, to please Michele a while, reminisces also about being sheltered beneath that cloak. Whereupon he lifts it and throws her upon her lover's body.

II: SUOR ANGELICA

We find ourselves in a convent in Italy at the close of the seventeenth century. Sister Angelica (soprano), banished to a convent for her love-child, misses the baby; her aunt appears to have her sign away her family claims and tells her that her son is dead and has been these past two years. Angelica is ruined by this news and takes poison but when, in her death throes, she prays to the Virgin, a celestial choir in radiant light occupy the chapel and on the threshold stand the Virgin and the child.

III: GIANNI SCHICCHI

It is Florence in 1299 and we are in the bedroom of Buoso Donati. He has just died. His relatives are anxious that he may have left his money to the monastery at Signa, especially in view of the roguish way in which it was acquired. They ransack the room, find the will, and find that he had indeed done so. They send for the equally roguish Schicchi (baritone) to help them. He will not help until he hears that his daughter's marriage with Rinuccio (tenor), a relative of Donati's, cannot proceed without a dowry. He sees his chance. He tells the relatives that he will impersonate Donati, as if on his deathbed, and dictate a will to a notary. An excellent scheme. It is put into action but the relatives are tricked, for Schicchi makes himself the beneficiary of the will. The relatives can do nothing and Schicchi chases them from what is now his house. He pleads with the audience: what better use of the money, than for the young lovers?

Futility Denied

In Italy things were, if anything, worse after the war than before. The mood was one of unrest as well as actual agitation. Puccini, almost a symbol of the elegant, old opera-going world with its firm social and sartorial hierarchy, despite his modest origins and his patchily achieved desire to work untouched by the din of the outside world, could no longer quite feel safe. In December 1918 he celebrated his sixtieth birthday. Three years later he moved from Torre to the coast, at Viareggio, not least to escape the peasant discontent – on one of his shooting excursions he was threatened by a local countryman. Events continued to unfold. The Fascist Party was formed in 1919 and there was frequent violence against the Communists; by 1921 there had been serious riots in Bologna, Florence and Milan. The King appointed Benito Mussolini Prime Minister in 1922 and within six weeks, in November, Mussolini was dictator.

For Puccini though, the immediate post-war task was to find a libretto.

Forzano, responsible for *Suor Angelica* (the composer's favorite of the triptych) and for *Gianni Schicchi* (the public's), worked on a play called *Sly*, which at the time both he and the composer considered for an opera. Adami was also called upon, along with a fine and distinguished writer called Renato Simoni (1875–1952), to construe elements of *Oliver Twist* into a libretto. Neither project came to anything, though it is interesting that Puccini was so drawn for the moment to English literature. (*Sly* came indirectly from Shakespeare.) Puccini liked London more and more, preferring it to Paris and admiring the enviable stability and sense of purpose of England after

Puccini – 'a symbol of the elegant old opera-going world' (AKG)

the war – at any rate, in comparison with rabblesome Tuscany. Equally however, such a context, as well as the Dickensian topics of social squalor, may also have had the opposite effect, driving him at last to desert 'reality' (let alone *verismo*) in favor of sheer magic and the truthful if not 'true' world of fable and even fairy-tale.

Once that had lodged in his mind, the fall of the dominoes seems straightforward: Simoni had written a play about Gozzi and had made a particular study of the eighteenth-century dramatist; from Gozzi's sheaf of fairy plays or, as he called them, 'dramatic fables', *Turandotte* stood out. (In 'Turandot', the last letter should be sounded.) The influence of the Venetian poet, writer and dramatist Count Carlo Gozzi (1720–1806) on the history of opera has been enduring: Mozart's *The Magic Flute* and Prokofiev's *The Love of Three Oranges* both come from fables published first in the early 1760s, and Puccini has not been the only composer to use *Turandotte*. A new, rather splendid edition of the Fables had appeared in Italy in 1884–5, in two volumes. As a yarn of the 'ice' Princess and the riddlesome triumph of love, it matched Puccini's most personal experiences – and his most Wagnerian yearnings.

Accordingly, research began, and by the autumn of 1920 the scheme of the opera had been agreed. This itself was some achievement, for not since *La Bohème* had the source for a libretto been so ramshackle as was the Gozzi, whose meandering plots and intricate subplots were almost the opposite of Puccini's requirements. What is more, the composer added to this elements not to be found in the original, notably the tragic Liù, whose suicide precipitates Turandot's comprehension of and transfiguring surrender to love.

Puccini had already started on the music. From then till his death, work continued, in an uneasy sway from total enthusiasm to bleakest despair. The

Count Carlo Gozzi: his collection of fairy tales and fables has provided plots for a number of operas (AKG)

librettists were of course caught in this storm – as late as in the autumn of 1921 he even talked of radically reducing the action from three acts to two (Gozzi has five); and that November, with the first act more or less finally complete, he even glanced at alternative schemes. This same pattern was repeated a year later. But by that time he was voicing his fears about ever finishing the piece.

Two theories present themselves, neither to be discounted nor either of them excluding the other. One is medical, the other artistic. For the first, it is simply that we are nowadays much more open to the idea that in a disease like cancer, mind and body are not at all out of touch; that no matter how unconsciously, he 'knew' of the mortal illness within him long before it was diagnosed just weeks before his death. This gives these mood swings and of artistic direction something of the character of a race against time. On the other hand, on the creative side of things, quite apart from the ever more plain new directions other composers were taking away from his lyrical tradition, it is clear from his notes at the time that the crucial passage of the opera, the kingpin of its deepest momentum, was the huge hymn to love's triumph that closes it, and this was exactly what Puccini's experience of love did not include.

Thus he found himself as Wagner had done more or less midway in *Siegfried*, the third of his 'Ring Cycle'. Required, by his own libretto, to set to music world-warming love, he found it could not be summoned from his experience, and (to put it all too briefly) he interrupted the composition of the tetralogy in order to write

An unusually clear and definite manuscript page from Puccini's desk, for Turandot *(Lebrecht)*

both *Tristan und Isolde* and *Die Meistersinger* in a process of investigation and discovery necessary to give him the insight he required. Puccini had the libretto of his third act in the summer of 1922, but it was a year before he really started to work on it. There can be no doubt that the final love duet and chorus to the triumph of love is of the utmost importance in the drama, not simply because of the very nature of such sentiments but also because the *transformation* of the Princess, into a woman rekindled in love, must be weighty and uplifting in a colossal manner. The complaint that this transformation – this *transfiguration* – happens too quickly after the suicide of Liù entirely misses the point: it is the sight of that tragic devotion that gives Turandot the power to triumph over the thirst for death that lovelessness has given her, and to open her soul to love itself. For once Puccini is not engaged in quixotic or esoteric *verismo*, but in something as fully symbolic as any of Wagner's allegories in which the veracity is to the truths of the soul rather than to everyday life. If we see the setting as purely as it should be, that is to say in the fairy-tale world of princes and princesses or the mythological world of symbols and significances, the dénouement is no more sudden or less affecting than the moment at the close of Wagner's *Lohengrin* at which, having been forced to reveal his name, the knight departs on the swan that collects him. Emotional and symbolic revelation dictate the timescale, not some paltry clock.

Puccini did not finish this music.

After March 1924 he achieved little work. His throat complaint and the ritual false diagnoses and irrelevant treatments, so common even today with cancer patients, gave him little time or energy for composition. The arrival of a final text of the final duet, in October, coincided with persistent pain and, by the end of the month, the generally agreed diagnosis of a tumor requiring treatment by x-ray. This of course was a treatment in its first days of development. Early in November he traveled from Viareggio to Brussels, which (with Berlin) was at the forefront of the technique. He began to suspect or to realize that *Turandot* would not be completed, yet he set off for the hospital with the manuscripts. He was to do no more work. After a week of the most ghastly treatment, his heart gave out, and on November 29 he was dead.

Toscanini appointed Franco Alfano (1875–1954) to complete the opera from Puccini's draft. At the first performance, at La Scala on April 26, 1926, Toscanini set down the baton at the point where Puccini had stopped, and told the audience that it had been here the master had broken off his work: 'Death on this occasion was stronger than art.' To hear that final duet, however, will tell us that longing defeats futility and that love is stronger than death.

In the final moments of
Turandot, *David Hockney
evoked the transfiguration of the
Princess through love by an
extraordinary enrichment of the
lighting as the chorus swells, seen
here in his working
model ©David Hockney.
Photographs by Richard Schmidt*

Turandot

We are in Peking, in legendary times.

Act I
Timur (bass) and his faithful servant girl Liù (soprano) find Calaf (tenor) in the surging crowd at the Imperial Palace. Timur is the deposed King of Tartary, Calaf his son; they must keep their identity a secret from the Chinese. The crowd hears of the imminent execution of a Persian prince who has failed the test of the three riddles which any suitor wishing the hand of Princess Turandot must pass. Silently, the Princess refuses to commute sentence, but Calaf gazes upon her and curses her cruelty in deep fascination. Three men-about-court, Ping, Pang and Pong (baritone, tenor, tenor), seek to persuade him of his folly, as do Liù and his father, but he is determined. He strikes the gong to announce his challenge.

Act II Scene I
In their pavillion within the palace, Ping, Pang and Pong lament the state of China and the carnage of Turandot's curse. They long for their country homes; and, for Turandot, true love.

Puccini's death mask (Lebrecht)

Act II Scene II

Inside the palace the scene is set for the three riddles. The Prince is not to be deflected: Turandot asks, and one by one Calaf correctly replies. The final riddle is answered by her name. She is distressed at her inevitable surrender, but Calaf says he will give his life if she can discover his name before dawn.

Act III

It is decreed that nobody should sleep till the stranger's name is found, and Calaf rests in a garden of the palace as dawn approaches. He looks ahead to kindling the Princess's love with a kiss. Ping, Pang and Pong attempt to seduce him to give his name but when Liù and Timur are brought in, it becomes clear that they will resort to violence. They threaten the old man but Liù declares that it is useless, only she knows his identity. She stabs herself. All are taken aback by this demonstration of devotion and as the Prince kisses the Princess she understands that his name is Love.

Ricordi's publication of the Turandot *libretto (AKG)*

Recordings of Puccini's Work

Although Edison had taken out his patents twenty–five years before, it was only in 1902 that the recording industry took its most significant first steps. In a suite in the Grand Hotel, Milan, Caruso recorded ten sides for the *Gramophone and Typewriter Company*; these took a couple of hours and the singer demanded £100 (approximately $150). Recordings had been made before, but these were the first to create an international market; they helped 'make' Caruso and Caruso helped the medium expand from its hitherto local scale. Those ten sides are still available today.

The repertoire of that session consisted of two arias each by Franchetti, Verdi and Boito, and one each by Donizetti, Massenet, Mascagni and, ninth in order, Puccini: 'E lucevan le stelle', from *Tosca*. Despite the woeful pianist and a wrong first note, Caruso's control is marvelous, from an even and restrained tone at first to an ever more impassioned outburst. The final sob is wonderfully vocalized, too; that is rare enough, for the histrionic sob was a stylistic lapse that set in early in the history of recording and has not left us. Puccini on record had made a good start.

That side is still available, most remarkably in the Pearl reissue of all of Caruso's recordings. This is on four chronological sets of three CDs each. The sound is unashamedly like that of a horn gramophone in a comfortable drawing-room, and this applies to the company's reissues of other singers, many singing Puccini excerpts and many, moreover, who were known to the composer. Other companies that specialize in this repertoire on CD are, most notably, Nimbus and Preiser. In general, Preiser has a restrained and careful sound to its transfers; the Nimbus

The composer's villa, standing on the edge of the lake (Lebrecht)

process on their Prima Voce series, while less hissy, is somewhat strident and hard, less of a drawing-room and more like an empty ballroom. Their compilations, however, both of Caruso and of other singers, have attractive selections.

Puccini is more or less the first opera composer to have had such close relations with singers who made records – though one of them, Tamagno, was the first Otello for Verdi – and even if you balk at the primitive sound quality, there is instruction as well as entertainment to be had here. Not least in the wild discrepancies of style. Take for instance Rodolfo's 'Che gelida manina' from the first act of *La Bohème*. Nobody today would sing it with the theatrical shifts of voice used by Giovanni Zenatello, opening with an air of startling diffidence, but going on, as he tells of his life, to a sort of mock grandeur. He was the first Pinkerton in *Madame Butterfly*, and though he made only two records from that opera, his discography is relatively rich in Puccini. Pearl have issued almost all of it, in two sets of four discs; the better of his two versions of Rodolfo's aria was made in London in 1908 and is in the first set. At the other extreme, however, try Fernando de Lucia; amongst other things he was London's first Cavaradossi (in 1900), but his languid two-sided version of the aria is unique, too. He allows ornamentation in a *bel canto* style even in those days a trifle outmoded, as well as time to laugh at the jovial conceit in the libretto, seldom noted, at the point at which the impoverished poet says, 'And how do I live? I live.' The pace here and in the rest of the scene (recorded a little later) is extremely slow, but winningly intimate and gentle.

That record, made in 1919 and reissued by Pearl in a set of three CDs of de Lucia's operatic recordings, was then one of many of that aria, reminding us that the sheer familiarity of such music was already a problem: singers strained to be

MADAMA BUTTERFLY

DE

G·PUCCINI

FANTAISIE
POUR PIANO PAR

CHARLES GODFREY JUNr

110877

G. RICORDI & C.
MILANO

ROMA - NAPOLI - PALERMO
LEIPZIG - BUENOS AIRES - S. PAULO
PARIS: SOC. ANON. DES EDITIONS RICORDI
LONDON: G. RICORDI & Co., (London) LTD
NEW YORK: G. RICORDI & Co. Inc.

(Copyright MCMVII, by G. Ricordi & Co.)

(Printed in Italy)   (Imprimé en Italie)

Lire 7.50

The frontispiece for a piano adaptation of Madame Butterfly, *1907 (AKG)*

different. Caruso had warned a rival, 'I am not a tenor to be copied,' but it is true of any great singer.

Sometimes the results were lamentable, sometimes glorious; sometimes in dispute – I for one adore Giuseppe Anselmi's bashful account of that aria, a Fonotipia of about 1907, but others may find it simply awkward or lumpy. Nor can one nowadays count on finding it at all: even on CDs, print-runs can be short and esoteric labels numerous as well as elusive. For our present purposes let me merely list some singers in the pre-LP era from whose Puccini excerpts I never cease to draw pleasure or elucidation.

With, if appropriate, a particular role, I would name, amongst sopranos: Margaret Sheridan (Butterfly), Rosetta Pampanini (Mimi, Butterfly), Göta Ljungberg (Tosca), Meta Seinemeyer, Salomea Kruszelnicka, Lotte Lehmann, Elena Ruszkowska (Tosca), and Selma Kurtz. Claudia Muzio made few records of Puccini, but there exists an air-check of a first act of *Tosca* from a live performance in the early 1930s; crackly as it is, the boldness and indeed Callas-like vivacity of the voice are impressive.

Nor, in that role, should we overlook Maria Jeritza: Rupert Christiansen tells the infamous story in his book *Prima Donna*:

Her most sensational effect came as Tosca. When rehearsing in Vienna with the composer, who admired her enormously, she fell accidently to the ground just before the 'Vissi d'arte', and discovering she had a nose-bleed, decided to stay there. Puccini approved the idea as a means of sustaining the dramatic impetus at a point where it is otherwise dissipated. Jeritza worked it up into a complicated piece of grovelling business, her hair falling over her face and her head sinking over her hands in a fit of sobbing.

'At first', wrote Lotte Lehmann severely, 'the effect was electrifyingly natural. Later on, however … that shock of hair always coming undone at precisely the same moment began to seem awkward and embarrassing because the artifice, the practised gesture with which she removed her hair-pins, became so obviously contrived.' Geraldine Farrar, herself a great Tosca, was ever terser; 'I obtained no view of any expressive pantomime of her pretty face, while I was surprised by the questionable flaunting of a well-cushioned and obvious posterior.'

Amongst tenors, I would name in addition to Caruso and the others mentioned already, Benjamino Gigli, Aureliano Pertile, Joseph Hislop, Tino Pattiera, Giovanni Martinelli, Giacomo Lauri-Volpi, Ettore Bergamaschi and Charles Kullmann. And of lower voices, Pasquale Amato, Giuseppe De Luca, Anafesto Rossi, Gerhard Hüsch and Mario Sammarco.

SNIPPETS

Of course, 78s are almost invariably of excerpts, though more or less complete versions of operas were surprisingly quick to appear; in 1918 *La Bohème*, in 1920 *Tosca*, in 1922 – in English, indeed – *Madame Butterfly*, with Rosina Buckman. We have to tolerate piecemeal documents for historical reasons, but the Puccini singer's skill is much less well represented by excerpts than, say, in Verdi, let alone Bellini or Donizetti. In general, recordings of excerpts are tolerable only where full versions of the works, or at least of the act, are unavailable. All the more frustrating therefore to have to recommend so strongly a disc issued by Nixa, giving four love duets: Lenora Lafayette, soprano, and Richard Lewis, tenor, sing with the Hallé Orchestra conducted by Sir John Barbirolli in the late 1950s. Barbirolli lingers, it is true, a common trait when the music is so familiar, and a trait frequently exacerbated by the circumstances of playing excerpts; here let me say simply that it is for once no fault, but an unleashing of the most irresistible music–making.

Occasionally single acts are available, few more satisfactory than the fourth act of *La Bohème* conducted by Sir Thomas Beecham; it was recorded at the time of performances at Covent Garden in 1935, and features the Rodolfo of Heddle Nash. The balance of correctness and passion is extraordinary and one wonders if there is any playing or singing like this nowadays.

Beecham's later recording of the whole opera (from 1956) was made in New York, with Jussi Bjoerling and Victoria de los Angeles; this is a great set, on EMI, Beecham's sense of point and sweep quite infectious. Still, the earlier act IV (on Pearl) conveys an ebbing entropy more movingly paced than in almost any other version.

PIRATES

This is the usual, but inaccurate, term for recordings taken mostly from broadcasts and issued legally on disc by independent companies. Such recordings can also often be found as gifts attached to the front of magazines, especially in Italy. Sometimes the sound quality is inferior, justified by something special in the

The frontispiece for a piano adaptation of
Turandot, *1926 (AKG)*

interpretation, but especially in the case of those coming with magazines the sound is usually fair to good.

We owe to this type of source at least half a dozen performances of *Tosca* with Maria Callas in the title role. They span nearly fifteen years, in other words more or less every phase of her voice; quite simply, they help us map the increase in dramatic detail and power that took place while the voice was in what is taken to be decline. She is best partnered by Tito Gobbi as Scarpia, especially in the second act, fearsomely conveyed, yet in each case with different nuance. If you find, say, the complete Covent Garden performance of January 24, 1964, on Melodram, conducted by Carlo Felice Cillario, in the second act you are pitched into an atmosphere more laden with risk and edge than could ever be achieved in the studio or with any other artists. This is helped by a particularly vehement account of Cavaradossi, here again with a heroic anger and defiance that will bring you to your feet.

Other performers best represented in such live recordings include, after Callas, perhaps most of all Magda Olivero, an extraordinarily under-rated soprano, a glorious Turandot in particular. As for *Turandot*, though not in the highest quality of sound, Leopold Stokowski's New York performance in 1961, with Birgit Nilsson, is almost my favorite, next to the EMI Callas recording. Franco Corelli hurls his way about as Calaf, Anna Moffo is touching as Liù, but I am always moved by Alessio de Paolis as the aged emperor, whose age and exasperation is quickly and affectingly conveyed.

Also from 1961, incidentally, comes Luciano Pavarotti's first great success, as Rodolfo, in a live performance of *La Bohème* given at Reggio Emilia. Francesco Molinari Pradelli conducts. This is one of Pavarotti's finest roles; the exuberance and dash suit him perfectly, and both here (Foyer) and in his studio recording (Decca) he carries all before. Some subtlety is missing, but the advantages greatly outweigh this. The studio recording is with Herbert von Karajan, whose longing for smoothness gives only a one-sided appreciation of Puccini's scoring. This is true but less damaging, by the way, of his *Turandot* (DG), in which the lushness has its place.

Callas

Complete recordings of *Manon Lescaut*, *La Bohème*, *Tosca* (twice), *Madame Butterfly* and *Turandot*, all with Callas, remain indestructible in the EMI catalogue. None can be ignored: for one thing, one has to take account of the dramatic flexibility of this voice, and its intelligence with regard to the texts over which, after all, Puccini spent so much time and energy. Decca has reissued performances of both *La Bohème* and *Madame Butterfly* with Callas's supposed arch-rival Renata Tebaldi, and the purity and singleness of tone in both performances are worthwhile, in the latter especially, but for what I call dramatic flexibility, so vital to Puccini's conception of theater and music, only Renata Scotto can be compared with Callas. Her Butterfly has Barbirolli conducting and Carlo Bergonzi as Pinkerton (on EMI), and is one of the most satisfying and lush versions that does not lose the rough edge of what is actually happening, in this perfectly unpleasant story, to an overall sheen.

Callas has spawned imitators even more ill-advised than those who flaunted Caruso's advice not to imitate him. One such was thought at the beginning of her career to be Nelly Miricioiu, and in her singing of *Tosca* on Naxos various patches of intonation and breathing hint at the homage, but the overall impression is quite different, especially in her understated way of suggesting the fragility of the character. Silvano Carroli gives Scarpia both charm and ruthlessness; Alexander Rahbari conducts (as he does in *Manon Lescaut* and *Madame Butterfly* on the same label), all performances of fresh and unaffected theatrical vigor.

CONDUCTORS

Scotto also recorded *Madame Butterfly* for CBS with Maazel a decade later than with Barbirolli. Maazel has since recorded almost everything of Puccini's, including *Le Villi*, *Edgar*, and *La Rondine*. Scotto features on the earlier recordings, and Domingo throughout, and for renderings on the sinewy side, both in style and in recording, these are admirable. Yet the proejct can be tied down just a shade by the completeness at stake, as if a sort of definitive worthiness induces a sense of duty or control at moments at which, in performance, adrenalin would raise the game of the interpretation.

This danger is proven by his live recording of *La Fanciulla del West*, made at La Scala in 1991. This is a fabulous reading, the soprano Marra Zampieri simply tremendous and heart-winning, while for once Domingo seems impassioned rather than professional. Perhaps Leonard Bernstein is to be singled out for making live performances acceptable commercially in a market ever bothered by 'perfection'. (He did record *La Bohème* with a young cast and at langorous tempi, but it did not survive in the catalogue.) At any rate, as with Bernstein's *Tristan und Isolde*, Maazel's

Ricordi's publication of La Bohème, *1900 (AKG)*

Fanciulla clinches the argument. Indeed, reservations I have always had about some of the score – such as the repetitive cowboys' 'Hello!' in the first act – pale beside the color and clarity and passion of it all.

Karajan is another conductor associated with Puccini's music but with him again the gleam and perfection simply sit ill with what is after all theater music. I find his *Turandot* most impressive, on DG, a recording in which Domingo's sometimes all-purpose ardor suits the character of Calaf quite well. The other parts are cast at a high level.

Barbirolli, so poorly represented in opera, features in an historical disc from EMI, in excerpts also from *Turandot* with Martinelli and Dame Eva Turner. This is again singing of extraordinary voltage. Perhaps nowadays the conductor who balances best the demands of raw sound and beauty is Giuseppe Sinopoli, whose *Manon Lescaut* and *Madame Butterfly* have been issued on DG. I still find that he has a tendency to shock, in which real outbursts of sound are too often gratuitously sudden, but since this is a more theatrical fault it is preferable to something more pious.

The Puccini Tuscany Trail

O nly one of Puccini's full-length operas – *Tosca* – is set in Italy; in Rome, indeed, a city the composer never lived in nor greatly cared for. His relationship with his native countryside, however, is an important aspect of his character and does find expression in his music. In both *Fanciulla* and *Turandot* especially there are lyrical episodes of homesickness that can seem to come from a deeper spring of inspiration than almost anything else in those scores; except, in the latter, that wistful triumph of love.

Tuscany is a province of many landscapes. The most usual scene that comes to mind may be of partly parched, partly lush low hills, peppered with cypress trees and faded ochre farmhouses. This is true of Tuscany to the south of the river Arno, but not of the north or by the sea to the west. The Arno drains into the Mediterranean through a wide basin of absolutely flat land – much of it marshland even today – demarcated along the north by immediately steep hills, and while Pisa straddles a slow bend of the Arno, Lucca lies at the northern edge of the basin, just before the hills rise to give an impressive sense of otherness and solitude. Indeed, these slopes are for the most part much less spoiled by building than one would expect and there are valleys just inland, away from the basin, so richly forested that the view is as if unchanged since Roman times.

Only in the last years of his life did Puccini move to the coast, at Viareggio, not least for the bracing, supposedly healthy air that seaside towns inspire. Perhaps he planned for his old age, since he bought the land long before he built on it. The

The statue of Puccini at the shore of Torre del Lago (J Brown)

The side-rear view of San Michele's theatrical false facade (J Brown)

greatest part of his life, however, was centered on Torre del Lago, now known as Torre del Lago Puccini, a mere three miles inland from Viareggio. At Torre, the composer faced the other direction, inland, but across the vast lake of Massaciuccoli towards those steep green hills of northern Tuscany. His house was on the very edge of the lake, perhaps five or ten yards from the water's edge; today, though, a piazza has been built in front of the house and the neighboring formerly waterside buildings, necessary perhaps for parking and for souvenir stalls but spoiling the romantic way in which, in his day, Puccini's house stood by the water like a boat on a beach.

However much may be read into his preference for an inward-looking settlement with his back to the sea, at the shore of a frequently sultry lake that separated him from the lush hills, as an indication of his melancholy, self-doubting and shy character, the fact remains that he relished the spot for its hunting and fishing. It is a region of unexpected contrast, unexpected because the seemingly monotonous flatness conceals the fact that as you cross it, the view can change abruptly according to the sightlines afforded by different levels of water and vegetation; and, once in the hills, there is an ever unfolding view back down to the lake and marshes. The simplest way to take in these little vista-dramas that meant so much to Puccini, is to drive between Lucca, Chiatri and Torre, in a zigzag or in a round trip, taking in as well, if you wish, Viareggio on the coast or Celle, the ancestral home of the Puccini family, in the hills a couple of miles north of Chiatri. In Celle – itself also slightly cunningly promoted sometimes as Celle Puccini – there is even a small museum to the composer's family.

In Lucca, of course, there is a museum at Puccini's birthplace in the via di Poggio (off from the piazza San Michele, opposite the church). The compact web of narrow

Puccini at Torre del Lago (Lebrecht)

streets of this proud town repays even the most aimless wandering as much as the most diligent sight-seeing. It becomes easy to understand how a single family might keep hold on the musical life of such a place for so long; equally easy to understand Puccini's need to escape. The composer was most associated with the cathedral of San Martino, as organist, and this building has one of the finest and quirkiest facades in Italy; but to get there from his home the young composer would always have scurried past the church of San Michele, with its theatrical false façade that makes the building out to be very much larger than it is.

Leaving Lucca to the north-east, Chiatri can be found in the hills that overlook the lake and beyond it the sea. Puccini lived here only while he was at work on *Tosca*, Elvira finding it far too secluded and soporific. Nonetheless, just to pass through it gives a fine perspective on the sort of hilly landscape the composer bought properties in for his shooting.

From Chiatri the easiest way to Torre is to carry on through the hamlet and down the folds of a valley (under the slender viaduct of the motorway), crossing the flatlands first to Viareggio; but only a little navigation and courage are needed to find a way across the marshes themselves on the long straight dusty roads that cannot have changed since the turn of the century. This grid of ditches and tracks maps out acres of tall reeds and grasses which make for an uncanny claustrophobic spaciousness.

Then at Torre, bisected by the old main road, turn inland at the main crossroads until you reach the lake: there is Puccini's house, now also the chief museum of his effects. There is also a summer festival here which, in 1994, celebrated its fortieth season, mounting productions in a theater built out over the lake. Lucca and Pisa

Puccini's birthplace from across the square, Lucca (J Brown)

also stage opera regularly. Opening times and facilities need to be checked from season to season, but the guidebooks and leaflets are helpful and in general information should be sought in the first instance from the Lucca Tourist Information Office: telephone (583) 491205 and 491689, facsimile 490766.

The composer's autograph and self-caricature on his notes for Vecchia Zimarra *(Lebrecht)*

Where appropriate, the name of the librettist(s) or author of the text is given in brackets. The date given is the date of completion and in some cases also the dates of first performance or production (FP) and/or of first publication (P).

BEFORE 1880: LUCCA

Organ music, various

Choral music, various

'Praeludio Sinfonico' for orchestra (1876)

Cantata, 'I Figli d'Italia bella' (1877)

'Motet' & 'Credo', (FP: Lucca 1878) (1878)

'Vexilla Regis prodeunt', for 2-part male chorus & organ (1878), (FP: Lucca 1878)

'Salve Regina', for soprano & harmonium

Mass for four voices & orchestra, 'Messa di Gloria' (1880), (FP: Lucca 1880) (P: 1951) (includes the earlier 'Motet' and 'Credo')

1880–1883: STUDENT DAYS, MILAN

Works for String Quartet (1880–1883):

Scherzo

Quartet in D major

Fugues

Songs with piano accompaniment:

Five settings of Ghislanzoni:
'Melanconia', 'Allor ch'io saro morto' (1881);
'Noi leggeremo', 'Spirto gentil' (1882);
'Storiella d'amore' (1883)
Romanza: 'Menti all'avviso' (Romani) (1883)
'Adagietto', for orchestra (1883)

'Capriccio Sinfonico', for orchestra (1883), (FP: Milan 1883),
(P: 1978); (arranged for piano duet by Giuseppe Frugatta, P: 1884)

'La Sconsolata' for violin and piano (1883)

1884–1892: The First Two Operas

Le Villi, opera in one act (FP: Milan 31 May 1884); revised version, in two acts (FP: Turin 26 Dec.1884), (Fontana)

Two Songs: 'Solfeggi' & 'Sole e amore' (1888)

Works for String Quartet (1889–1890):
2 Minuets
'Crisantemi'

Edgar, opera in four acts (FP: Milan 21 April 1889);
revised version, in three acts (FP: Ferrara 28 February 1892), (Fontana)

1893–1924: THE MATURE COMPOSER

Manon Lescaut, opera in four acts (FP: Turin, 1 February 1893),
(Leoncavallo, Praga, Oliva, Illica, Giacosa)

La Bohème, opera in four acts, (FP: Turin, 1 February 1893),
(Giacosa & Illica)

March, 'Scossa elettrica' (1896)

'Cantata a Giove' (1897)

Cantata, 'Inno a Diana', for orchestra & piano (1897), (Salvatori), (P:1899)

Marching song, 'Avanti, Urania!', for chorus & piano (1899), (Fucini), (P:1899)

Song, 'E l'uccellino' (1899), (Fucini)

Tosca, opera in three acts (FP: Rome 14 January 1900), (Giacosa & Illica)

Song, 'Terra e mare' (1902), (Panzacchi)

Madame Butterfly, opera in two acts (three scenes), (FP: Milan 17 February 1904; revised version Brescia 28 May 1904), (Giacosa & Illica)

Requiem, for chorus & organ (or harmonium), in memory of Verdi (1905)

Two pieces for piano (1910), (P: 1942):

Foglio d'Album

Piccolo Tango

La Fanciulla del West, opera in three acts (FP: New York 10 December 1910), (Civinni, Zangarini)

La Rondine, opera in three acts (FP: Monte Carlo 27 March 1917), (Adami)

Song, 'Morire?' (1917), (Adami)

Il Trittico, three one-act operas; (FP: New York 14 December 1918):

Il Tabarro (Adami)
Suor Angelica (Forzano)
Gianni Schicchi (Forzano)

Turandot, opera in three acts (FP: Milan 25 April 1926), (Adami, Simoni)

The following list of recordings is included as a guide to some of the interpretations of Puccini's work available at the time of writing and is by no means intended as an exhaustive catalog. The works are listed first, followed by details of the recording, the artists, record company and disc number. All numbers given are those that apply to the compact disc format, but many recordings can also be bought on conventional tape cassette.

OPERAS

LA BOHÈME

Callas, Di Stefano, Moffo, Manerai, Zaccaria, La Scala, Milan, Ch. & Orch, Votto.

EMI mono CDS7 47475-8.

De los Angeles, Bjoerling, Merrill, Reardon, Tozzi, Amara,
RCA Victor Ch. & Orch., Beecham.
EMI mono CDS7 47235-8.

Tebaldi, Bergonzi, Bastianini, Siepi, Corena, D'Angelo, Ch. & Orch. of
the Accademia di Santa Cecilia, Rome, Erede.
Decca 440 233-2.

Carreras, ROHCG Ch. & PO, Davis.
Philips 416492-2.

Freni, Pavarotti, Harwood, German Opera Ch., Berlin,
Berlin PO, Karajan.
Decca 421 049-2.

La Bohème: Act IV only

Nash, London PO, Beecham.

Pearl GEMM CD 9473.

EDGAR

Scotto, Op. Orch. of New York, Queler.

CBS M2K 79213.

La Fanciulla del West

Zampieri, Domingo, Pons, La Scala, Milan, Ch. & Orch, Maazel.

Sony Dig S2K 47189.

- RECOMMENDED RECORDINGS *of* PUCCINI -

MADAME BUTTERFLY

Callas, Gedda, Borriello, Danielli, La Scala, Milan,

Ch. & Orch, Karajan.

EMI mono CDS7 47959-8.

Tebaldi, Bergonzi, Cossotto, Sordello, Ch. & Orch. of the Accademia di

Santa Cecilia, Rome, Erede.

Decca 440-230-2.

Scotto, Ambrosian Op. Ch., Philharmonia Orch., Maazel.

CBS M2K 35181.

Freni, Carreras, Berganza, Pons, Ambrosian Op. Ch.,

Philharmonia Orch., Sinopoli.

DG Dig. 423 567-2.

MANON LESCAUT

Callas, Di Stefano, Fioravanti, La Scala, Milan, Ch. & Orch, Serafin.

EMI mono CDS7 47393-8.

Freni, Domingo, Bruson, ROHCG Ch. & PO, Sinopoli.

DG Dig. 413 893-2.

Gauci, BRT PO, Rahbari.

Naxos 8.660019-20.

LA RONDINE

Te Kanawa, Domingo, Nicolesco, Rendall, Nucci, Watson, Knight,

Ambrosian Op. Ch., LSO, Maazel.

CBS M2K 37852.

IL TRITTICO

Scotto, various Orch., Maazel.

CBS M3K 79312.

TOSCA
Callas, Di Stefano, Boggi, Calabrese, La Scala, Milan,
Ch & Orch, De Sabata.
EMI CS7 47175-8.

Miricioiu, Czecho-Slovak Radio Symphony Orch.
(Bratislava), Rahbari.
Naxos 8.660001-2.

Vaness, Philadelphia Orch, Muti.
Philips 434 595-2.

Caballé, Carreras, Wixell, ROHCG Ch. & PO, Davis.
Philips 412 885-2.

TURANDOT

Callas, Fernandi, Schwarzkopf, Zaccaria, La Scala, Milan, Ch. & Orch,
Serafin.
EMI mono CDS7 47971-8.

Nilsson, Corelli, Scotto, Mercuriali, Giaiotti, Rome Opera Ch. & Orch,
Molinari-Pradelli.
EMI CMS7 69327-2.

Ricciarelli, Domingo, Hendricks, Raimondi, Vienna State Opera Ch.,
Vienna Boys Ch., Vienna PO, Karajan.
DG Dig. 423 855-2.

TOSCA: EXCERPTS

Eva Turner, Martinelli, Albanese, Favero, Tomei, Dua, ROHCG Ch.,
London PO, Barbirolli.
EMI mono CDH7 61074-2.

LE VILLI

Scotto, Domingo, Nucci, Gobbi, Ambrosian Op. Ch., National PO,
Maazel.
CBS MK76890.

OTHER WORKS

MESSA DI GLORIA

West German Radio Ch. & Symphony Orch., Inbal.

Philips 434 170-2.

SONGS

Domingo.

Sony Dig. SK44981.

EXCERPTS

LA BOHÈME

MADAME BUTTERFLY

Farrar.

Pearl. GEMM CD 9420.

CARUSO IN ENSEMBLE

Nimbus. Prima Voce. NI 7834.

ANTONIO SCOTTI

Pearl. GEMM CD 9937.

FERNANDO DE LUCIA

Operatic Recordings 1902–21.

Pearl. GEMM CDS 9071.

The Era of Adelina Patti

Nimbus. Prima Voce. NI 7840/1.

Caruso Edition

Pearl EVC I, II, III, IV.

Covent Garden 1904-39

Nimbus. Prima Voce. NI 7819.

Love Duets

Lafayette, Lewis, Hallé Orch., Barbirolli.

Nixa NIXCD 6005.

Giovanni Zenatello:

The Complete Recordings.

Pearl. GEMM CDS 9073/4.

The catalysts of a writer's work are always numerous, though the faults always his or her own; let me however express my thanks first of all to David Nice, who set the project in motion, and my editor Emma Lawson, who kept it (and myself) on the rails.

Without Nicole Proetta I should have understood and seen and loved rather less as I worked.

Most of the actual writing was done at the home of Don and Pam Stevens at Montauroux, where the view of Var country made me think of the Tay, if not Tuscany; their indefatigable hospitality is as memorable as their ploy of having me mallet rocks as 'recreation' from my desk.

Also, thanks to Dushyant and Lois Patel, who welcomed my frequent invasion of their computer, to transform ink-blots to disk-bytes.

James, Gabriele and Alexander Rose looked after me wonderfully in Barga, in northern Tuscany, as a base for exploring both Puccini country and the generous batches of recordings I had received.

Any lover of music, let alone of Puccini's, brought up in Scotland in the 1960s, 70s and 80s, owes Sir Alexander Gibson a lifelong ovation for life-lasting memories of extraordinary performances; I treasure especially his *Madame Butterfly*, in which sound became blood and music the heart.

I also owe to working with David Hockney a deeper realization of what is at stake in *Turandot*, and indeed in art and opera themselves.

Nor have I forgotten my debt to Michael Tanner.

But if I may, I dedicate this to the memory of Dave Morgan, who knew and could weep for joy ...

AAM *Academy of Ancient Music*
arr. *arranged/arrangement*
ASMF *Academy of St. Martin-in-the-Fields*
attrib. *attributed*
bar. *baritone*
bc. *basso continuo*
bn. *bassoon*
c. *circa*
ch. *chorus/choir/chorale*
Chan. *Chandos*
cl. *clarinet*
CO *Chamber Orchestra*
COE *Chamber Orchestra of Europe*
comp. *composed/composition*
contr. *contralto*
db. *double bass*
DG *Deustche Grammophon*
Dig. *digital recording*
dir. *director*
ECO *English Chamber Orchestra*
ed. *editor/edited*
edn. *edition*
ens. *ensemble*
fl. *flute*
HM *Harmonia Mundi France*
hn. *horn*
hp. *harp*
hpd *harpsichord*
Hung. *Hungaroton*

instr. *instrument/instrumental*
kbd. *keyboard*
LSO *London Symphony Orchestra*
Mer. *Meridian*
mez. *mezzo–soprano*
ob. *oboe*
OCO *Orpheus Chamber Orchestra*
orch. *orchestra/orchestral/orchestrated*
org. *organ/organist*
O–L *Oiseau–Lyre*
perc. *percussion*
pf. *pianoforte*
picc. *piccolo*
PO *Philharmonic Orchestra*
qnt. *quintet*
qt. *quartet*
ROHCG *Royal Opera House, Covent Garden*
sop. *soprano*
str. *string(s)*
tb. *trombone*
ten. *tenor*
tpt. *trumpet*
trans. *translated/translation*
transcr. *transcribed/transcription*
unacc. *unaccompanied*
va. *viola*
var. *various/variation*
vc. *cello*
vn. *violin*

- SELECTED FURTHER READING -

Arthur M.Abel, *Talks with Great Composers* (New York, 1955)

Giuseppe Adami, ed., *Epistolario* (Correspondence), trs. Ena Makin (London, 1931)

Alan Blyth, ed., *Opera on Record* I–III, (London, 1979, 1983, 1984)

Mosco Carner, *Puccini: A Critical Biography* (London, 1958;1992)

Rupert Christiansen, *Prima Donna* (London, 1982)

C. Hopkinson, *A Bibliography of the Works of Giovanni Puccini* (New York, 1968)

Spike Hughes, *Famous Puccini Operas* (London, 1959)

Spike Hughes, *Great Opera Houses* (London, 1956)

The Earl of Harewood, ed & rev., *Kobbé's Complete Opera Book* (New York, 1922 etc.)

G. Marek, *Puccini. A Biography* (New York, 1951)

Ernest Newman, *More Opera Nights* (New York, 1954)

Stanley Sadie, ed., *The Grove Dictionary of Music*, 6th edition (London, 1980)

Michael Scott, *The Record of Singing* (London, 1977)

- ACKNOWLEDGEMENTS -

The publishers wish to thank the following copyright holders for
their permission to reproduce illustrations supplied:

Archiv Für Kunst und Geschichte, London
Lebrecht Collection
Private Collection, Lebrecht Collection
The Mansell Collection Ltd

1. LA BOHÈME, 'CHE GELIDA MANINA' 4'47"
   José Carreras
2. LA BOHÈME, 'SÌ. MI CHIAMANO MIMÌ' 4'52"
   Katia Ricciarelli
3. LA BOHÈME, 'O SOAVE FANCIULLA' 4'13"
   Katia Ricciarelli/José Carreras
   Orchestra and Chorus of the Royal Opera House, Covent Garden/Sir Colin Davis
   Here at the close of Act I Rodolfo touches Mimi's hand, so cold in the dark, and in
   (1) and (2) they exchange their histories before joining the others outside,
   which they do in their happy duet, lost in each other (3).

4. LA BOHÈME, 'QUANDO ME'N VO' 5'00"
   Ashley Putnam, Orchestra and Chorus of the Royal Opera House,
   Covent Garden/Sir Colin Davis
   At the Café Momus in Act II, Musetta seeks to attract Rodolfo's attention
   with this verse telling of how, when she walks down the street,
   she is the focus of everyone's attention.

5. LA BOHÈME, 'O MIMÌ, TU PIÙ NON TORNI' 5'30"
   José Carreras/Ingvar Wixell, Orchestra and Chorus of the Royal
   Opera House, Covent Garden/Sir Colin Davis
   Now in the final act, Rodolfo, the poet, and Marcello, the painter, intertwine
   their reminiscence of the lost happy days (Acts I and II); Rodolfo thinking of
   Mimi's beauty and of the fragility of their youth and love, and Marcello finding that
   no matter what he seeks to paint, Musetta's face always appears on the canvas.

6. **MADAMA BUTTERFLY, 'BIMBA, BIMBA, NON PIANGERE' (LOVE DUET)** 16'50"
Katia Ricciarelli/José Carreras, London Symphony
Orchestra/Lamberto Gardelli
This love duet is one of the most sweeping and touching rushes of passion in Puccini's output – a perfect example of his achievement in giving Italian opera a sense of seamless momentum learnt from Wagner.

7. **TOSCA, 'RECONDITA ARMONIA'** 3'37"
José Carreras, Orchestra and Chorus of the Royal Opera House,
Covent Garden/Sir Colin Davis
In his painting Cavaradossi has portrayed the face of the Marchesa Attavanti as the Mary Magdalene, and here in an impromptu moment standing back from his canvas, he sings of the 'rarified harmony' of Tosca's beauty in comparison to that of the Marchesa.

8. **TOSCA, 'AH, QUEGLI OCCHI'** 5'80"
Montserrat Caballé/José Carreras, Orchestra and Chorus of the Royal
Opera House, Covent Garden/Sir Colin Davis
The lovers pour out their feelings for one another – a mood which is briefly broken by Tosca's jealousy of the painting; Cavaradossi must explain that, in contrast to the Marchesa's eyes, none in the world are as beautiful as Tosca's.

9. TOSCA, 'TE DEUM' 4'34"

Ingvar Wixell, Orchestra and Chorus of the Royal Opera House,
Covent Garden/Sir Colin Davis
At the close of Act I, the Te Deum is beginning, while Scarpia's thoughts turn to Tosca who, he believes, will let him into her heart.

10. TOSCA, 'VISI D'ARTE, VISSI D'AMORE' 3'33"

Montserrat Caballé, Orchestra and Chorus of the Royal Opera House,
Covent Garden/Sir Colin Davis
In Scarpia's room, Tosca – rejected by Cavaradossi for her betrayal; desired by Scarpia – laments the harmlessness of her life of love and art before this sorry episode.

11. TOSCA, 'E LUCEVAN LE STELLE' 3'16"

José Carreras, Orchestra and Chorus of the Royal Opera House,
Covent Garden/Sir Colin Davis
Act III: in the final hour before his execution, Cavaradossi has permission to write a letter, but his thoughts turn to the evenings of delight he spent with Tosca.

12. TURANDOT, 'NESSUN DORMA' 3'01"

José Carreras, Royal Philharmonic Orchestra/Roberto Benzi
Here at the opening of the final act, the unknown Prince Calaf echoes the Empress's order that 'nobody shall sleep' while they seek to discover his identity before daybreak. He knows that it will fall to him to reveal his name and at that moment he and his love shall triumph.